# New Ways in Teaching Adults

Marilyn Lewis, Editor

**New Ways in TESOL Series II**
Innovative Classroom Techniques
Jack C. Richards, Series Editor

TESOL

Teachers of English to Speakers of Other Languages, Inc.

Typeset in Garamond Book and Tiffany Demi
by Capitol Communication Systems, Inc., Crofton, Maryland USA
and printed by
Pantagraph Printing, Bloomington, Illinois USA

Teachers of English to Speakers of Other Languages, Inc. (TESOL)
1600 Cameron Street, Suite 300
Alexandria, Virginia 22314 USA
Tel 703-836-0774 • Fax 703-836-7864 • e-mail publ@tesol.edu • http://www.tesol.edu

Director of Communications and Marketing: Helen Kornblum
Managing Editor: Marilyn Kupetz
Copy Editor: Cheryl Donnelly
Cover Design: Ann Kammerer

TESOL thanks Barbara Jacobson, the staff, and the students at Northern Virginia Community College, Alexandria, Virginia, for their assistance and participation. TESOL also appreciates the cooperation of Michael Carrier, the staff, and the students of Eurocentres, Alexandria, Virginia.

ISBN 0-939-791-68-4
Library of Congress Catalogue No. 96-061905

# Contents

# Acknowledgments

My thanks are due to all the teachers who have contributed to the book either willingly or as a result of many months' coercion. Thank you for taking the trouble to pass your good ideas on to colleagues all over the world, despite the reservations many of you expressed about whether anyone would be interested in your modest idea. Contributions have come in from Canada and the United States, Great Britain, the Middle East, Asia, South Africa, Australia, and, of course, New Zealand, where people found it harder to escape from my relentless appeals.

Thank you also to the many people who had good intentions, conveyed to me by fax and e-mail but who didn't quite make the deadline. Perhaps yours will be ready for another book in the series. Finally, I would like to thank the University of Auckland for allowing this project to be part of my leave proposal for the third term in 1995, and Dorothy Brown, who took my place so well that many people may not even have noticed that I was away.

# Introduction

Other books in this series have collected ideas for particular aspects of language teaching such as vocabulary and reading. Many people, when approached to make contributions for this volume said, "But how do I know if my idea is really new?" In encouraging them to write down an idea that was new for them or for their class and that had improved their students' learning, I suggested that newness is in the eye of the reader. If an idea has been developed to suit one group of students somewhere in the world and has worked well with them, the chances are that somewhere else there is a teacher who will also enjoy using it and find it innovative.

This book brings together contributions from teachers in as many countries and parts of the world as possible and from classrooms where students have many different reasons for learning English.

## *Classifying the Tasks*

A book with the word *new* in its title has the chance to do more than describe individual tasks. It can also introduce teachers to new ways of looking at those tasks. In selecting chapter headings, I rejected the traditional divisions of reading, writing, speaking, and listening as the basic organizational unit, partly because these divisions would overlook the integrated nature of many of the tasks. Another reason was that separate books have already appeared in the series for each of them. One way of categorizing tasks would be according to some of the headings used in books of communicative activities: ranking, classifying, jigsaw, and so on. Apart from the fact that these divisions have been used very effectively already, many of the ideas that teachers sent in would not have fit into these headings.

Other ways of classifying tasks would be by the level of difficulty, the form of student grouping, the amount of teacher intervention, and the degree of reality. Levels would have been straightforward because the teachers all supplied these (beginning, low intermediate, and so on), although several mentioned a range of levels. The form of class grouping (pairs, small groups, the whole class) didn't seem a significant point, particularly as some tasks can be done in more than one way or change their grouping as the activity moves along. Some measures of task, such as the amount of teacher intervention and the degree of "reality," depend on a continuum and are therefore unsuitable for sections of a book.

From an editing viewpoint, either the categories had to be those supplied by the contributors, or the editor would have to go through them all trying to read beneath the surface and picture how they would appear from the students' perspective, using the description provided. The tasks arrived with information about levels, the type of class, the aims, resources and procedures—categories that correspond roughly to the key components of tasks identified by Nunan (1993): goals, teacher and learner roles, settings, activities/procedures, and input data.

Classification according to goal would be a logical one and easy to identify. Two objections came to mind. The first is that one task can have many goals, and the second is Kumaravadivelu's (1993) point that there can be a mismatch "between teacher intention and learner interpretation of language learning tasks" (p. 83). What is revision for some students is almost like meeting new language to others whose memories of yesterday's lesson are less sharp.

Focusing on learner roles seemed a more innovative classification and one that could let teachers look at what the learners were actually doing in a new light. However, extracting the many possible roles in each activity from the procedures listed seemed artificial as well as cumbersome. Nor did the procedures fall into tidy categories. The many examples showed "a great deal of overlap and interdependence between the various types of activity" (Legutke & Thomas, 1991, p. 34).

Finally, I chose the category of input data as the basic organizational unit of the book, hoping that it would alert teachers to the range of sources available as prompts for lessons at any level.

## *Types of Input*

Perhaps as a reaction to earlier times when input (from the teacher and the text book) dominated the learning process, input, as a distinguishing feature of tasks, has not had much attention in the two decades of communicative language teaching. Input is "what functional language and means of expression a learner must have in order to participate productively in a communicative task" (Legutke & Thomas, 1991, p. 61), taking for granted that all the tasks that follow are communicative in the broadest sense of the word.

The types of input required for the tasks in this book range from the formal input of direct teaching to language collected by students in out-of-class tasks. They include print, graphics, and sound. Some are open-ended, in the form of stimuli that lead students to recall language; others are complete texts. Some have been created by the teacher while others come from the students and from "authentic" sources. The type of input is the organizing unit finally chosen for this book.

## References and Further Reading

Crookes, G., & Gass, S. M. (Eds). (1993a). *Tasks and language learning: Integrating theory and practice.* Clevedon, England: Multilingual Matters.

Crookes, G., & Gass, S. M. (Eds). (1993b). *Tasks in a pedagogical context: Integrating theory and practice*. Clevedon, England: Multilingual Matters.

Legutke, M., & Thomas, H. (1991). *Process and experience in the language classroom*. London: Longman.

Kumaravadivelu, B. (1993). The name of the task and the task of naming: Methodological aspects of task-based pedagogy. In G. Crookes & S. M. Gass (Eds.), *Tasks in a pedagogical context: Integrating theory and practice* (pp. 69–96). Clevedon, England: Multilingual Matters.

Nation, I. S. P. (1990). *Language teaching techniques* (Occasional Paper No. 2). Wellington, New Zealand: English Language Institute.

Nunan, D. (1993). Task-based syllabus design: Selecting, grading and sequencing tasks. In G. Crookes & S. M. Gass (Eds.), *Tasks in a pedagogical context: Integrating theory and practice* (pp. 55–68). Clevedon, England: Multilingual Matters.

# Users' Guide to Activities

## Part IV: Direct Teaching

## Part V: Worksheets to Complete

## Part VI: Word Prompts

## Part VII: Nonverbal Stimuli

## Part VIII: Task Instructions

## Part IX: Other People

## Part X: Case Studies

**Part I: The News**

*Kimbunda Mwasa Jolie at Northern Virginia Community College, Alexandria, Virginia USA.*

# Introduction

Newspapers, radio, and television broadcasts have the advantage of being topical, cheap, and easily available, at least in English-speaking countries. In this section, teachers show ingenuity in the number of ways they use the media to increase students' language learning in context, to make links between the world they live in and other places, and to teach skills of independent reading.

# Radio News

**Levels**
Intermediate

**Types**
General English

**Aims**
Summarize information
from written and
spoken sources
Recognize and
reproduce the
conventions of a radio
news broadcast

**Class Time**
2–2½ hours

**Preparation Time**
None

**Resources**
Current newspaper (one
copy per group)
Radio
Tape recorders and
audiotapes (one per
group)

In this activity, students summarize and rank the international and national news from several sources. Students then work together, under deadline, to produce their own radio broadcasts using current news sources.

## Procedure

1. Ask the class to imagine that they all work at the local radio station. The station starts broadcasting in 2 hours. The telex and fax machines have broken down, so they have to prepare a news broadcast using all the resources they have (newspapers and radio broadcasts from other stations) by the time the station goes on the air in 2 hours' time.

2. State that the broadcast must be 3 minutes long, and the students will need to:
   - rank the stories
   - decide how much time to put into each story
   - write the text
   - practice the broadcast before they record

3. Elicit and put on the board the conventions of the radio news, for example:

   | | |
   |---|---|
   | station and speakers' names | time |
   | introduction | headline |
   | stories | weather report |
   | summary of stories | time of the next broadcast |
   | name of the station | |

4. Have the students start by ranking and summarizing the stories in the newspaper.

5. After about half an hour, invite one or two elected members from each group out of the room to listen to the news on the radio from another station. Have the students listen once, make a summary together, and then take the summary back to their groups. (If you tape the news while the students are listening to it, you can have them listen to the broadcast more than once.)

6. Have groups then incorporate new updates and fresh news into their rankings and summaries.

7. Give regular time reminders, and ensure that everyone in the groups is working on some aspect of the task.

8. Half an hour before the deadline, tell the learners they have to be ready to perform within 15 minutes so that they have time to practice, review, and edit. Remind them of the radio news conventions.

9. Have each group perform and record the broadcast. Make sure each group finishes recording in time to listen to an actual news broadcast.

10. Play each of the recordings to the class, asking them to compare the ranking of the stories, the conventions, and tone of the recordings.

## Caveats and Options

1. Have students revise and record again their broadcasts after making comparisons to other broadcasts.

2. Have students create listening tasks based on their recordings for use by other groups or classes.

3. Extra work can be done on the differences between written and spoken speech.

## Contributor

*Averil Coxhead has taught in New Zealand, Estonia, Hungary, Romania, and England. She is currently teaching at Victoria University, Wellington, New Zealand.*

# Making Our Own News

**Levels**
Low intermediate +

**Types**
Any

**Aims**
Practice using direct and
indirect quotations in
context correctly and
accurately
Develop fluency and
accuracy in question
making
Use all four skills
creatively

**Class Time**
2 hours +

**Preparation Time**
5 minutes

**Resources**
Article from a
newspaper that clearly
uses quotations from
one or more sources
News headlines from
stories in brief from a
newspaper
Newspaper stories in
brief (optional)

This activity gives learners the chance to practice interviewing someone and then write a report of the interview using quotations. Learners act both as journalists exploring a story and as eye-witnesses recounting another story. This activity also raises learner awareness of the contextual knowledge readers and writers bring to the text as the stories are created merely from a suggestive headline.

## Procedure

1. Choose a short newspaper article, put the headline on the board, along with the people, places, and key words mentioned in the article. Have learners make up a story combining all these elements and tell their versions to others in small groups.
2. Have students read the original article silently to determine whose story was the closest to the original.
3. Have students discuss the main ideas, use of quotations, and structure of the original text in groups.
4. Elicit the procedure journalists go through to write stories (e.g., receiving a tip, making contacts, thinking of questions to pose, interviewing several sources, correlating the information, and writing the story). Put these steps onto the board.
5. Tell the learners they will be following the same procedure both as journalists and witnesses using brief headlines they have been given by their editor-in-chief (you). Their job is to get the story ready for the next edition of the paper in 2 hours' time.
6. Put the news headlines on the board. Divide the class into an even number of small groups. Have each group select a story they would like to investigate.

7. Have the groups write 10 questions they will ask as journalists when they interview witnesses. It is important that all the members of the group contribute and have a copy of the questions they create. Ask them to put aside the questions until they conduct the interview.

8. Ask one learner from each group to write the group's headline on a piece of paper and then exchange their headline with another group.

9. Tell the learners that this new headline is the basis for a story in which they have been involved. They have to create the story as a group, assigning themselves roles and characters, as they will be interviewed about what happened.

10. To set up the interview situation, have each student pair off with a member of the group with whom they exchanged headlines. Have one person act as the journalist using the questions created earlier and the other act as the witness, using their story and character invented earlier. The journalist takes notes during the interview, being careful to take at least two exact quotes. The interviewee needs to be careful to stick to the story the group invented, as many diversions from the story will distort the report.

11. Have the interviewer and interviewee change roles at the end of the first interview and conduct the second interview.

12. Regroup the learners. Explain that they are now at the correlation stage of the process. They have to get all the information they have gathered individually to work into a story to go to press in the next edition of the paper. They must include at least one sourced quotation from each person interviewed—direct or indirect.

13. Give students time and encouragement to get the story written but also remind them that the deadline time is coming up and they need to have the copy ready by then. It helps to assign a secretary to do the writing. Reluctant participants can be given jobs such as checking the quotations, looking for loop holes within the stories, working on the linking of ideas, or ensuring that the stories contain all the important ideas.

14. Have each group report on their story to the class. The stories can then be checked and put on the wall for everyone to read.

## Caveats and Options

1. It is essential that the learners create the story together so that they can give a coherent account during the interview. It also helps if the learners define their roles in the story so that they have a clear idea of how to answer the questions and quotable statements to give.
2. Any misquotes can be the subject of Letters to the Editor the following week.
3. The stories can be compared with the original briefs if the learners are interested.
4. The interviews can be performed in front of a video camera or a microphone and presented in documentary style.
5. The stories can be put into a front page or newspaper format with the class deciding on layout, pictures, and so on. Publishing the texts looks professional and can be done easily on computer by the learners.
6. The stories can be used as reading, viewing, or listening material for other classes.
7. Role plays can be created and performed using the situations that arise.
8. This activity can be used for radio and television media as well if the equipment is available.

## Contributor

*Averil Coxhead has taught in Estonia, Hungary, Romania, England, and New Zealand. She is currently teaching at Victoria University, Wellington, New Zealand.*

# Learner Training in Listening Skills

**Levels**
Intermediate +

**Types**
Semester courses for
adult immigrant learners

**Aims**
Develop listening skills
such as predicting,
listening for the main
idea and details
Learn vocabulary in
context
Be informed about
world news

**Class Time**
30 minutes on two or
three occasions, about a
week apart

**Preparation Time**
15 minutes or less on
two or three occasions

**Resources**
Tape recorder
Audiotape of the day's
*BBC World News*
Worksheet or blank
paper

Newly arrived immigrants wish to keep in touch with world news and yet are often prevented from doing so by their lack of vocabulary and listening skills in English. The format of the *BBC World News*, with its headlines, news items, and main points, is ideal for teaching the listening skills necessary to give students access to this information. The skills practiced (predicting, listening for main idea and details) are important for these learners to develop. They can be transferred to all types of listening—social listening, listening to lectures, and listening to instructions at work.

## Procedure

1. Discuss with learners the news broadcasts or telecasts they listen to. Do they listen to any other radio and TV programs? How much do they understand?
2. Tell learners you are going to show them ways in which they can increase their level of understanding and also improve their listening skills.
3. Introduce the *BBC World News* and its structure—headlines, news items, and main points.
4. Have students note on their worksheets the names of countries in the world that are currently in the news. Write the list on the board. Discuss how they might know when one news item ends and another begins.
5. Have learners listen and count the items as you play the headline or the main points. Play again and ask them to write the names of the countries featured in each item.
6. Discuss the benefits of having predicted the countries first. Was it easier to hear them?
7. Ask how they might know which are key words in a listening text.

8. Play one headline or main point again. Have learners write down any words that they hear and understand that seem to be important.

9. Write the words that learners offer on the board. Put learners in groups or pairs and have them guess from the key words the main idea of the item.

10. Have students listen again for more detail and pick out more words. How did predicting from key words help them to hear these new words?

11. Play the audiotape a final time and ask specific questions, encouraging learners to focus on the key words that could provide the answers to the questions. Teach any new vocabulary.

12. For homework over the following week, ask learners to record further news broadcasts and use the above technique to get the gist of the news. Have students give oral reports to the class on news items they have heard.

13. Repeat the activity one day a week for the next 2 or 3 weeks, gradually reducing the number of preparatory steps and reviews as they become more proficient.

14. After the last session, discuss ways of using the skills they have learned in other contexts, such as listening to conversation or lectures, watching TV programs, and following instructions at work.

**Caveats and Options**

1. Other types of news broadcasts could be used in a similar way. Learners can progress to listening to local news and TV news in larger samples as their knowledge of the local context grows.

**Appendix: Sample Worksheet for Listening to the News**

A. How many items are there on today's news?

B. Write down the country and, if possible, the main topic of each news item:

1. _____
2. _____
3. _____
4. _____
5. _____
6. _____

C. Choose an item and write the main idea.

D. Write here any important new vocabulary you wish to learn from today's news.

**Contributor**

*Heather Denny is senior lecturer in the School of Languages, Auckland Institute of Technology, in New Zealand, where she has taught English to immigrants for many years.*

# What's in a Headline?

**Levels**
Intermediate +

**Types**
Students who do not
regularly read a
newspaper in their L2

**Aims**
Identify idioms and
colloquialisms used in
everyday conversation
by native English
speakers
Become aware of the
condensed nature of
newspaper headlines

**Class Time**
30–45 minutes

**Preparation Time**
1 hour

**Resources**
One or two newspapers
Handout of current
newspaper headlines
and overhead
transparency (OHT)
explaining headlines

Intermediate and advanced students are often keen to hone their skills in English with a knowledge of current idioms. As many of the phrases in present use have not been included in dictionaries yet, newspapers are the most readily available source—particularly the headlines.

## Procedure

1. Give out the handout of headlines. Pair off students.
2. Put up the OHT of explanations and read these through.
3. Ask students to find an idiomatic expression or a colloquialism on the handout corresponding to each of the explanations on the OHT.
4. Have each pair expand one or two headlines into a full sentence.
5. Ask students to try to think of the origin of any of the expressions. Find out if they have an equivalent in their L1s.

## Caveats and Options

1. Select the headlines from one recent newspaper.
2. When cutting out the headline, include some of the smaller print text as a clue to meaning.
3. Encourage students to bring along headlines that could be used for future discussion.

## References and Further Reading

Grundy, P. (1994). *Newspapers*. Oxford: Oxford University Press.

## Contributor

*Noelene Evans teaches ESL at Otago Polytechnic, Dunedin, New Zealand. She has taught other languages in high schools in New Zealand.*

# Know How You Listen

**Levels**
Advanced

**Types**
Any

**Aims**
Explore the memory
processes utilized while
listening
Identify alternatives for
effective information
processing

**Class Time**
1½ hours

**Preparation Time**
1 hour

**Resources**
Short local news stories
with transcripts
Good audiotape
playback system
Worksheets

Students who need help in listening often have misconceptions about how they should process rapidly delivered condensed information as in news reports. They tend to attribute their poor listening to their short memory span and regret that they cannot attend to each word uttered and recall word for word. Little do they realize that failing to chunk information or attend to the overall message may be the culprit. This activity raises students' metacognitive awareness of their listening behavior and helps them explore alternative ways of processing information.

## Procedure

1.  Inform students that effective listeners use different ways to process incoming information, for example: attending to key words as indicated by prominence of stress within an information unit, attending to ideas and observing the relationships among them as indicated by transitional/discourse markers, and attending to the overall content and trying to make sense of it using their own experiential knowledge.
2.  Tell students that they will be going through some recorded authentic listening materials to explore their own listening processes and to identify strategies for improvement.
3.  Make the specific learning objective explicit to the students and clearly explain the steps they are expected to go through in achieving the objective. Emphasize that in this activity, it is their listening behavior rather than their comprehension ability on which they should focus primarily.
4.  Help students learn how to identify their listening processes. Demonstrate what you mean by listening behavior by working through one short recording with them. It might be helpful to invite a student to help you demonstrate.

5. Prepare worksheets (see Appendix) with both the objective and instructions clearly stated for reference. Design them so that students can use them with their own listening materials for further practice. Transcripts should be made available for reference.

6. Conclude the session by encouraging learners to seek ways to improve their information processing.

## Caveats and Options

1. A variety of short and coherent audio recordings with familiar subject matter should be made available to students. Minimize the negative effect of visual distractions and unfamiliar topical knowledge.

2. Apart from asking students to examine their own listening process, you may invite them to compare their processes with those of their friends to explore alternatives.

3. Follow-up sessions may be conducted to help students learn more alternatives in managing information.

## References and Further Reading

Rost, M. (1990). *Listening in language learning*. London: Longman.

## Appendix: Sample Worksheet

Objective:    Explore the memory processes we experience while listening.
Text type:    News broadcast
Activity:     Recall, note-taking, and summary writing
Level:        Advanced

Part I

1. Choose a short news broadcast with a familiar topic.
2. Listen to the selected news story without taking any notes on the first attempt.
3. Jot down as much key information as you can recall immediately after listening. (You may use language, pictures, or graphics for your purpose.)

*Reflections*

1. What came to your mind immediately when you first tried to recall the news story? Sounds? Words? Sentences? Picture? Image? Scene(s)?
2. Look at the key information you noted down after the first listening. What kind of information is it? Key words? Short phrases? Sentences? Names? Ideas? Images? Pictures?
3. What does this kind of information show about your listening?

Part II

1. Listen to the same news broadcast a second time.
2. Take notes (in any form) while listening with the aim of writing a summary of the news story.
3. Write a summary of the news story based on the notes taken.
4. Read through the full transcript of the news story and evaluate your summary.

*Reflections*

1. Look at the notes you have taken after the second listening. What kind of information is it? Is it similar to or different from the kind you recalled after the first attempt?
2. Explain the similarity or difference and account for it. Did you attend to the incoming information differently in both attempts? How?
3. What have you learned about how you listen based on the recalled information, notes taken, and the summary you have written? Ask yourself questions such as:
   - Do you generally attend to every word you hear or to key words?
   - Do you listen for the idea first before you take notes, or do you take down whatever you can hear?
   - Do you try to make sense of what is happening in the news by using imagination and world knowledge? If so, how?
   - Do you rely on a particular habit of listening rather than using a combination of different strategies in processing information?

*Self-Assessment*

1. Read through the transcript of the news story and assess your summary. Have you covered the main points coherently? Is any key information omitted?
2. What overall problems do you have in writing the summary? Is it just a recall problem or has it got something to do with how you listen?
3. How would you approach listening and summary writing tasks in the future?

## Contributor

*Jose Lai has taught ESL at the tertiary level for more than 10 years. She is currently a PhD candidate at the School of English and Linguistics and Media of Macquarie University, Sydney, Australia.*

# What's the News?

**Levels**
High beginning-
intermediate

**Types**
Adolescents and adults

**Aims**
Practice question forms
Paraphrase and retell
information

**Class Time**
25-40 minutes

**Preparation Time**
Minimal

**Resources**
Newspaper clipping(s)
Chalkboard or
whiteboard and pens

In this activity, new settlers have a chance to keep informed of the local, national, or international news that interests them while practicing new language skills. Where possible use the news from the students' home countries for high interest and motivation. Use newspapers from students' home countries, if available, as these are likely to contain additional information.

## Procedure

1. Write a news headline on the board. Divide the board into three columns after the news headline.
2. Ask if students know what the news could be about. Teach new vocabulary as necessary.
3. Have students form *wh-* questions to get information about the news item. (To help beginners, write down *Who? What? Where? Why? When?* and *How?* on one side of the board).
4. Write students' questions in Column 1. If the question is incorrect, invite correction from the student or from the class. Write corrections in Column 2. Invite the student to repeat the question using the correct form. Check pronunciation.
5. Write the answers to students' questions in Column 3. (See below.)

| Your questions | Your questions corrected | Answers |
|---|---|---|
| Is it a study of the night? | ✓ | No, it's about studying at night. |
| Who has fear? | Who is afraid? | Women students. |
| What are they afraid? | What are they afraid of? | Being attacked in the dark. |

6. When enough essential information has been gathered, summarize the news using the notes on the board, pointing to each one as it is used. Repeat this summary two or three times.

7. Ask the students to have a turn in retelling the news, using the teacher's model or in their own way. Use the more able (or confident) students first. The less able students can be asked to have a go when they have heard the story many times over. (This is a free practice; do not overcorrect syntax or pronunciation).

**Caveats and Options**

1. Make sure as many students as possible take a turn.
2. The more able students can be given the news items (or bring their own) and act as facilitator.
3. A small group can be given the news item and share the job of answering the questions from the class (always making sure of the correctness of the form).
4. After this initial oral work, the original text can be read together with the class and extra information added to the summary.
5. High frequency or new vocabulary can be learned when used in context without referring to the bilingual dictionary.
6. Students can write the story for homework. The grammatical errors can be used as teaching points in follow-up sessions.

**Contributor**

*Kim-Hoang Macann is an ESOL teacher trainer in Christchurch, New Zealand. She is currently a school adviser on cultural and ESOL matters in the northern parts of the South Island of New Zealand.*

# Environmentally Sound

**Levels**
High intermediate +

**Types**
Private language school
or language institute
International English
Language Testing Service
(IELTS)

**Aims**
Skim for main points
and discussion
Practice intensive
reading and note-taking
with problem-solution
texts
Practice verbal
summarizing and
information exchange

**Class Time**
50–60 minutes

**Preparation Time**
5 minutes (for
photocopies)

**Resources**
Photocopies of three
newspaper reports on
environmental issues

The activity can be used within the framework of a topic-based series of lessons on the environment. It is neither the first nor the last in this series. It can be integrated with a video or other recorded listening exercise on the same topic.

## Procedure

1. Brainstorm on the problems, solutions, and causes of air pollution.

2. Have students choose or you distribute copies of three newspaper articles on environmental issues. Make sure that each article is read by an equal number of students. Following a 2–3 minute reading, ask students to form groups with the other students who read the same article to compare the content (and structure) of the article.

3. Next, allow 15 minutes for intensive reading and (individual) note-taking for the following points: problems, causes, solutions, and problems with solution. Pair off students and have them compare notes, amend their notes as necessary, and help each other with difficult lexis. Be available for consultation.

4. Regroup students into threes, one student for each article. Have students exchange information from their notes, not the original texts. The other students listen, question, and take notes.

5. Ask the class for feedback. Have students compare the situations described with those in their own countries and put forward proposals for the ideal and the most practical solution to the problems.

## Caveats and Options

1. Step 5 above could lead to some sort of written activity, or the whole activity could be an initial scenario for a larger scale project.

## Contributor

*Gavin Melles teaches at a private language school in Auckland, New Zealand. He has taught foreign languages and EFL at different levels in New Zealand and overseas. He is currently completing a DPhil in linguistics at Waikato University.*

# Newspapers for a New Life

**Levels**
Low intermediate +

**Types**
High school
University
Adult education

**Aims**
Explore current cultural
issues of interest
Read contemporary
English
Prepare and deliver
formal oral
presentations

**Class Time**
15–30 minutes

**Preparation Time**
None

**Resources**
Current local or national
newspapers

Students can have the chance to evaluate their peers during informal presentations. Because the content is already there, they can concentrate on organizing and presenting skills.

## Procedure

1. Begin by explaining the purposes of this assignment:
   - to choose and discuss with the class a current topic of interest
   - to read an English language newspaper article
   - to prepare and deliver an oral presentation.
2. Model the assignment:
   - Prepare an overhead transparency or a large poster with the title of the newspaper article and a picture illustrating the article. (It is very important that the students learn to speak with an illustrated visual aid to support the presentation.)
   - Give a short summary of the article.
   - Prepare some questions to stimulate class discussion.
   - Conduct a metacognitive exercise for the class to analyze what you have done so that "student teachers" understand how to prepare the assignment. They may not simply read the article. They must summarize it in their own words and include some discussion questions.
3. Assign student teachers for at least the next month. Perhaps schedule this activity only once or twice per week.
4. Move to the back of the room while the student teacher takes over the class. As the student teacher is speaking, take notes for written feedback. The feedback can consist of an informal running commentary on the presentation or can take the form of a presentation check list (see Appendix).

## Caveats and Options

1. Do not allow a student to simply read from the article. Should a student test your determination, ask him or her to sit down and request proper preparation of the assignment for the next class. If you are not strict about this, you risk subjecting the class to a semester of incomprehensible mumblings.

2. Insist that the students identify the sources of their articles and that the newspaper be a recent edition. For example, you might accept publications from the previous 7 days only.

3. Inform the students that missing the student teacher assignment will result in a failing grade for that component of the class. Suggest that the students exchange telephone numbers to ensure that substitutes can be found in case of an emergency.

4. It is very important that you move to the back of the room so that the student teacher will address the class and speak with enough volume for everyone to hear rather than hold an intimate conversation with you.

5. If you are planning on giving holistic feedback, it may be helpful to assign at least one student evaluator to provide additional reactions by using the checklist in the Appendix.

6. Assign this as a required but ungraded exercise in order to foster a more relaxed atmosphere.

## References and Further Reading

Fenholt, J. S. (1988). *Ready to read*. Cincinnati, OH: South Western Publishing.

Fenholt, J. S. (1988). *Ready to read* (Teaching kit). Cincinnati, OH: South Western Publishing.

## Appendix: Sample Feedback Checklist

Name of Student Teacher:_____ Date_____

Title of newspaper article: _____

Name of evaluator: _____

| | Yes | No |
|---|---|---|
| Was the student teacher prepared? | ___ | ___ |
| Did the student teacher have a visual aid? | ___ | ___ |
| Did the visual aid contain the name of the article? | ___ | ___ |
| Did the visual aid have a picture? | ___ | ___ |
| Was the source of the article mentioned? | ___ | ___ |
| Was the source current? | ___ | ___ |
| Did the student teacher read the  presentation? | ___ | ___ |
| Did the student teacher summarize the article? | ___ | ___ |
| Did the student teacher prepare questions? | ___ | ___ |
| Did the questions stimulate discussion? | ___ | ___ |
| Did the student teacher make eye contact with the class? | ___ | ___ |
| Could the student teacher be heard? | ___ | ___ |

In general this presentation was:

excellent _____          acceptable _____          unacceptable _____

## Contributor

*Dorothy Solé has taught ESL for many years, both in academia and in the workplace. She lives in Miami, Florida, in the United States.*

# It's Your Story

**Levels**
Intermediate +

**Types**
Adults

**Aims**
Read a newspaper in
English regularly
Practice summarizing
Ask and answer questions
about newspaper stories

**Class Time**
20-30 minutes to explain
the project; 10-20 minutes
a day thereafter

**Preparation Time**
Daily time spent scanning
the newspaper for
interesting, topical stories

**Resources**
English language news-
papers (enough for the
entire class the first day)
TV schedule to locate
news times and channels
Newspaper for each
student throughout the
course (if possible)
Mailboxes (folders) for
each student

When students make their own news stories to discuss in class, they have a commitment to the discussion. This activity involves students during and outside class.

## Procedure

1. Initiate a discussion of reporting and following a story by asking students about reporters on popular television shows (e.g., *Murphy Brown, Lois and Clark*). Ask students questions to prepare them to follow a story themselves, for example:
   - How does a newspaper decide who covers what story? (It is usually assigned and/or area of specialty or interest for the reporter.)
   - What stories do you find most interesting? (Elicit categories such as world news, human interest stories, famous people, politics, business.)
   - What news story or issue have you found most interesting since you have been in this country?
2. Have students look through the first page of their newspaper to see which articles they find most interesting. Have students rate the articles (1, 2, 3) according to their interest. Ask them to put a star (*) next to the ones that are likely to be continuing stories.
3. As homework, have students watch one local news and one national news report. Go over times and channels in sample TV schedules.
4. Ask students to list the major stories reported and bring their list to class with them the next day. The purpose of reading, listening, and thinking about the stories is to select and follow one story that they find interesting.

5. Give students over the weekend to look for more news stories. Tell students to choose a news story to follow. Ask that they provide you with the topic of their story and at least one complementary newspaper article with citation.

6. Approve topics and conference with students to make sure that nobody has the same story, that they know of newspapers from which to select stories, and that stories are appropriate. Select a story to follow yourself.

7. Go over citation format. Make sure students list citations on their articles.

8. List and distribute everyone's topic (including yours) and put up individual mailboxes for everyone in the class.

9. Ask that students look for articles related to their own and other people's stories and also for articles that would be of use to others, using mailboxes to deliver and receive articles.

10. Once students have had some time to locate two or three articles, begin daily oral and/or written summaries of stories. You should also be a participant.

11. Ensure that class members or groups listen and ask questions of the story's reporter. Prepare a transparency of the more confusing or difficult articles and follow up the summary and question/answer period the next day with guided reading of the article.

12. Have students prepare and hand in a scrapbook of the most useful articles found, arranged in chronological order.

## Caveats and Options

1. If this is part of the students' class grade, you may ask that they put useful articles for others first into your mailbox with a note saying who it is from and who it is for so that you can give them credit for locating articles for others.

2. If you have a discussion or speaking focus to your class, consider assessing the student's oral article summaries (see Appendix A). Help them with problem utterances and give suggestions to help them to improve.

3. You may focus more on written summaries and ask that students not only put the articles into a scrapbook but also write a summary of

each article as they go. Go over summary writing techniques and use criterion-referenced grading (see sample in Appendix B) and process writing to improve the summaries. Students provide a citation at the top and key words going from general to specific at the bottom of each summary.

4. This project can also evolve into a consideration of audience, bias, and point of view of newspapers, with students asked to compare and contrast the same story as reported by two different newspapers.

5. Connect the project with Internet use in which students go onto the World Wide Web to locate stories from newspapers written in the target language.

6. For a reading focus, ask that students highlight their articles, focusing on thesis and major premises for a persuasive article and on *who, what, where, when, why,* and *how* for an informative article. Score ability to correctly highlight important information and work with transparencies and guided reading to improve skills.

## Appendix A: Sample Oral Article Summary Grade Sheet

Name _____

\_\_\_/ 5 Citation

\_\_\_/10 Thesis or topic

\_\_\_/10 Description of how the story has progressed/developed

\_\_\_/10 Main Points

\_\_\_/10 Useful examples, details included

\_\_\_/10 Language use and syntax

\_\_\_/10 Use of audience organizers

\_\_\_/10 Fluency/Pronunciation

\_\_\_/ 5 Preparedness

\_\_\_/10 Ability to respond to questions

\_\_\_/10 Knowledge gained

_____/100 TOTAL

Problem Utterances

Notes/Suggestions

## Appendix B: Sample Written Article Summary Grade Sheet

Name _____

____/ 5 Full citation provided

____/ 5 Citation in proper format

____/10 Indication of author's thesis

____/10 Main points identified

____/20 Main points summarized clearly

____/10 Summary organized and logical

____/10 Appropriate examples or details given

____/20 Language use

____/10 Mechanics (spelling, punctuation, handwriting)

| +2 | -2 |
|---|---|
| Indication of writer's purpose and audience | Unbalanced regarding main ideas and details |
| Overview of article's organization | Borrowed heavily from article |
| Review comments and criticisms | |

_____ TOTAL

## Contributor

*Kim Hughes Wihelm taught ESL in Hong Kong and Malaysia and is currently the intensive English program curriculum coordinator and assistant professor of linguistics at Southern Illinois University, Carbondale, in the United States.*

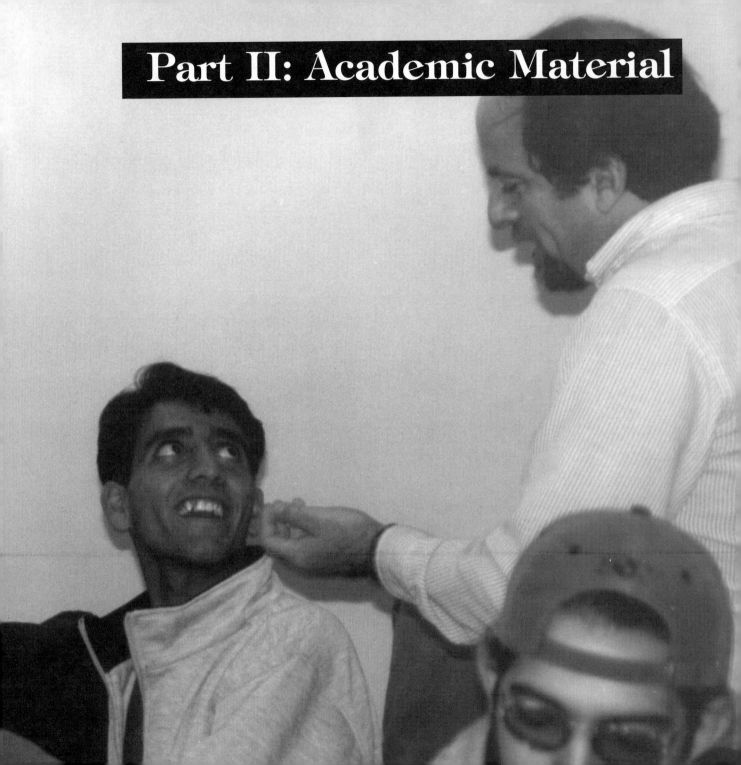

# Part II: Academic Material

*Mohammad Fayyaz and Arthur Perlstein at Northern Virginia Community College, Alexandria, Virginia USA.*

# Introduction

In this section, teachers describe activities for classes studying English for academic purposes (EAP). Their varied suggestions include analysis of written text and graph reading as a part of more general academic reading, and note-taking from lectures either through direct teaching or through learning from other students. Several activities bring together skills in listening, reading, speaking, and writing.

# Encouraging the Horse to Drink

**Levels**
High intermediate +

**Types**
Technical and Further
Education (TAFE)
vocational preparation
course with similar
amounts of English and
vocabulary modules

**Aims**
Skim and scan for detail
Take responsibility for
learning
Become familiar with
assessment criteria for
vocational assessment

**Class Time**
$1\frac{1}{2}$ hours

**Preparation Time**
1 hour

**Resources**
Relevant section of
syllabus for vocational
module
Vocational textbook or
other required reading
Worksheet

Second language students in vocational courses are often required to deal with large amounts of reading in complex language. They may attempt to cope with this by working longer and harder rather than working more strategically. They can focus their effort more effectively if they (a) think critically about what is necessary in order to meet course requirements; (b) use reading skills to enable them to ignore sections that are not accessible and focus on key areas; and, (c) prepare for vocational lectures by prereading.

## Procedure

1. Ensure that students have a copy of the vocational syllabus at the beginning of the course.

2. Ask students to read the learning outcome(s) and assessment criteria for the relevant section of the syllabus. Check for understanding.

3. Give students about 3 minutes to skim the relevant chapter of their textbooks and decide which sections need to be read, possibly read, or ignored.

4. Give students 5–10 minutes to go through the textbook again in more detail, matching chapter sections to learning outcomes/assessment criteria and marking these on their copies of the syllabus.

5. Hand out the worksheet (see Appendix). Ask students to scan the text for the listed words and then read to find the meanings.

6. Mark the words and discuss them in class, drawing attention to cues used in scanning and how meaning was located.

**Caveats and Options**

1. This activity works well with a clearly written, competency-based syllabus for which students have clear assessment information. Some adaptation may be required where other syllabus forms are used.
2. Cooperation with the vocational teacher is important for access to relevant materials and coordination of prereading with vocational lectures.
3. This activity assumes preteaching of:
   - textbook layout and use of text features in scanning (e.g., italics, subheadings, margin notes)
   - language structures used for definitions and explanations (e.g., *which*, dash, apposition).

**References and Further Reading**

Carvan, J. et al. (1995). *A guide to business law.* Sydney, Australia: Law Research Publications.

## Appendix: Sample Worksheet for Reading *A Guide to Business Law*

Chapter 17: Negotiable Instruments

1. Skimming for an overview:

   Check the Assessment Criteria for this section of the course.

   Skim through chapter 17. What sections do you think you need to read? Why?

   We are going to focus on checks. Is there key information you need from other sections?

2. Scanning for specific information:

   In which sections will you find information on each of the Assessment Criteria?

   Use section headings and margin notes to help you.

3. Guessing word meanings from context:

   What do the following words and expressions mean? Do not use a dictionary.

| | |
|---|---|
| 17.2 | negotiable |
| 17.3 | negotiable instrument |
| | delivery |
| | endorsement (see also 17.10) |
| 17.13 | stale cheque |
| 17.14 | converted |
| 17.16 | payable to bearer |
| | payable to order |
| 17.17 | holder in due course |
| 17.22 | renunciation |
| | material alteration |
| | forge (vb) |
| 17.23 | countermand |
| | signatories |

## Contributor

*Marion Bagot teaches ESOL at Hornsby College of TAFE in Sydney, Australia.*

# Videos for Note-Taking Practice

**Levels**
Advanced

**Types**
Weekly tutorial for EFL students enrolled in a university degree program

**Aims**
Learn that there are patterns to lectures
Improve listening and note-taking skills to save time and enhance learning

**Class Time**
50 minutes

**Preparation Time**
1 hour

**Resources**
Videotaped lectures
Worksheets

Students enrolled in a university degree program may find it difficult to complete both their degree coursework and EFL classwork. This activity helps students and the EFL teacher integrate the learning of content with developing skills or strategies.

## Procedure

1. Make students aware that listening to lectures is a skill and that, like other language skills, it can be learned. Tell them that lectures follow a limited set of patterns and that even jokes are part of the pattern. Explain that the class will be analyzing videotaped lectures in order to learn those patterns and use them to improve listening and note-taking.
2. Watch a videotaped lecture with the class. Concentrate on one point per session. For instance, in the first session practice noting when the lecturer moves from one subtopic to the next. Stop the video to talk about all the signals that illustrate a change. Notice words and phrases, change of intonation, gestures, pauses, and moving around. Later sessions can concentrate on summary statements, examples, asides, and so on.
3. Work through one tape together, highlighting the first change of topic and gradually involving the class.
4. Prepare worksheets (see Appendix) so students can practice individually, ticking and crossing off key words according to whether they think they hear a new point or simply an example of the previous one. After each tutorial, have the videotape and worksheet available for individual practice in the laboratory or self-access center.

**Caveats and Options**

1. This activity requires that about half a dozen lecturers, professors, or other colleagues agree to being videotaped as they give actual lectures.

**References and Further Reading**

Nattinger, J. R., & De Carrico, J. (1992). *Lexical phrases and language teaching.* Oxford: Oxford University Press.

## Appendix: Sample Worksheet for Listening to Lectures

1. Watch the first 5 minutes of the lecture on the videotape.
2. Stop, rewind, and watch it again.
3. Stop the tape each time you come to one of the sentences below.
4. Put a letter after each sentence to show its purpose:
   a. announcing a main point
   b. emphasizing a point
   c. changing from one point to another
   d. relating a point with something else
   e. introducing an example
   f. summarizing a point
5. Check your answers with the answer sheet.

Sentences From the Lecture

1. First we need a reasonable knowledge of . . .
2. As far as I'm concerned, that is your most important skill.
3. If you remember, we saw some examples of . . .
4. You need a system for this skill.
5. This next part refers to your handout.
6. Right now. Back to the basics.
7. In patient assessment, we have a two-tier assessment.
8. I remember the same thing happened to me during that big storm last winter.
9. OK. Now, what's the priority?
10. So the main thing in all this is . . .

Answer Key

1a  2b  3e  4a  5d  6c  7a  8e  9a  10f

## Contributor

*Hazel Chan tutors at the University of Auckland, in New Zealand, where she completed a Diploma in English Language Teaching. She has taught ESOL in Singapore and New Zealand.*

# Be Your Own Judge

**Levels**
Intermediate +

**Types**
General or academic
writing classes

**Aims**
Analyze features of good
texts
Judge own texts

**Class Time**
1½ hours

**Preparation Time**
Time to select an
appropriate text and
prepare the worksheet

**Resources**
Model text selected
from authentic material,
a text book, or student
work
Worksheet

Students of academic writing need to be introduced to a variety of genres—recount, argument, and so on. By analyzing samples, they discover features to use in their own writing.

## Procedure

1. Select a text that exemplifies qualities of the text type or genre. A good recount text (a text that explains a past event), for instance, may have a clear sequence of events, time markers, clearly identified characters, and consistent past tense usage. A good argument text may have a clearly stated opinion or thesis and clearly explained and elaborated reasons in support of the main thesis or idea. Derewianka (1990) lists the six major texts types or genres useful in teaching writing and provides clear examples of each genre and how it can be analyzed.

2. Prepare the worksheet grid and insert the model text (see Appendix A).

3. Have students circle the features of the text that they feel make it effective and write the reasons for their choices in the column beside the model text.

4. Have students write the same type of text or genre but on a different topic.

5. After writing, ask students to check their own text against the features listed in the column on the worksheet. (See Appendix B for an example.)

## Caveats and Options

1. This activity relies on a text that illustrates qualities of the text type or genre.
2. Analyzing the model text can be done individually, in pairs, or in groups.
3. Generally some preparation for writing should be included in the sequence after the text analysis and before the writing. For instance, for recount texts the speaking technique 4/3/2 is a useful precursor to writing. Students practice saying their recount to one partner for 4 minutes and then change partners and say their recount in the period of 3 minutes. On the third and final occasion, students again change partners but speak for only 2 minutes. (See Appendix C for an example of a sequence of tasks.)

## References and Further Reading

Derewianka, B. (1990). *Exploring how texts work.* New South Wales, Australia: Primary English Teaching Association.

Franken, M. (1993). Getting the most out of speaking activities that prepare students for writing. *Guidelines, 15*, 45-53.

Nation, I. S. P. (1989). Improving speaking fluency. *System, 17*, 377-384.

Rego, M. (1987). Adaptation of "Filling the bin." *School Journal, 1*, 3. (Wellington, New Zealand: School Publications)

## Appendix A: Worksheet With a Sample Analysis

| Circle the things you think are good in the text below. | What makes this a good recount text? Write your reasons below. |
| --- | --- |
| Mum and Dad are doing up our house. They keep pulling out old rotten bits and putting in new bits. It's going to look good one day but right now there's a lot of rubbish.<br><br>"We can't go on like this," said Mum. "We need to hire a bin."<br><br>"OK," said Dad. "I'll get one for the weekend."<br><br>On Friday, some men came and parked a big dumper bin on the | |

road outside our house. It looked enormous.

"We'll never fill that," we said.

"You'll be surprised," said Dad.

That night the bin was empty. The next morning there were things in it— cardboard boxes, old sacks and broken bricks.

"Someone else has put rubbish in our bin," we said.

"If I find out who did it," said Dad, "I'll dump it on their lawn." But he didn't know who it was, so we left it in the bin.

We spent a lot of time on Saturday hauling rubbish from our house and dumping it in the bin. By night time it was nearly full.

"We'll fill it up tomorrow," said Dad.

On Sunday morning we looked at our bin. It was only half full!

"Who's taken our rubbish?" we asked.

"Someone must have wanted it," said Mum. "Maybe they took the wood for their fire or the bricks to make a path."

So then we had room in the bin for lots more rubbish. We went on hauling and dumping all day. When we had finished late that afternoon, Dad called the people who hired the bin. "You can come and take

| the bin away now," he said. "And you'd better hurry. Someone keeps taking things out and putting things in."<br><br>    "That's what always happens," they said. |  |

Adapted from a story by Marion Rego (1987). Used with permission.

## Appendix B: Student Text Written After Doing the Worksheet

One difficulty of English for me is its pronunciation, especially the vowels and the sounds *s* and *th*. I caused an incident because of it. An exchange student lived near my house. We sometimes took the same bus and train to go to school. After having gone back to the USA, he wrote a letter to me. Having got it, I was very happy and brought it to school and showed it to a British teacher. She asked me, "How did you get to know him?"

I thought I answered, "In the morning, we took a bus together sometimes."

But the teacher looked very surprised and her face turned red and she asked me if this was true. I couldn't understand why she was so surprised. She asked me, "Yoko! You were taking a bath with him in the morning?"

I had mispronounced *bus*, saying *bath* instead. When we discovered my mistake, we burst out laughing. But I was also a little embarrassed. I blushed at the same time.

How difficult English is! Now I'm trying not to use "take a bus." I'm careful to use expressions like, "get on a bus" or "hop on a bus" instead.

## Appendix C: Sample Sequence of Activities

Writing Recounts

Task 1: Reading

Read the recount text below. What makes it an interesting text for you to read? Fill in the reasons. The reasons become the criteria for your own writing.

Task 2: Note-Taking

Choose one interesting event that happened to you recently or back home. Make a few notes to help your remember what you will say in the next task.

### Task 3: Speaking

Explain that event to your partner for 4 minutes.
Change your partner. Now explain the event in 3 minutes.
Change your partner one last time and explain the event for 2 minutes.

### Task 4: Writing

Now you're ready to write your text. After you've finished, check your own text against the criteria in Appendix A.

## Contributor

*Margaret Franken has taught writing skills classes in a wide variety of situations and has taught courses in writing pedagogy. She is a lecturer at Massey University, in New Zealand.*

# Different Subject—Different Style

**Levels**
Advanced

**Types**
University setting;
students of English for
academic purposes

**Aims**
Identify an academic
writing style
appropriate to own
subject area by
becoming aware of the
specific ways in which
language is used in that
area
Discover what can be
done outside the
classroom to aid
learning

**Class Time**
30 minutes

**Preparation Time**
None

**Resources**
Library containing
academic texts within
the students' subject
areas

Learners need to see subject-specific examples of academic writing, yet one English for specific purposes class may have students from several disciplines. Here, the class is involved in selecting appropriate texts for themselves.

## Procedure

1. Have a brief discussion with the class on different writing styles. Show how different subject areas use language differently. Identify an area of language (e.g., verbs, connectors, citation) that the students can work on.
2. Send the students to the library and ask them to find a text in their subject area that can act as a model of the writing style they want to achieve.
3. Have students photocopy a sample of the text (one or two pages), then highlight all occurrences of the area of language they are working on.
4. As homework, ask students to write a short piece of text using at least 50% of the highlighted words, then bring the photocopied sample and the piece of writing to the next class.
5. Pair off students with similar subject areas. Have them look at each other's writing and the photocopied samples and discuss their work.
6. While students are discussing, join at least some of the pairs briefly.
7. Ask students to rewrite their text using their peer's comments if they wish.
8. Have students submit their rewritten work for your comments and assessment.

## Caveats and Options

1. To suit different teaching schedules (and levels of motivation) this activity could be conducted entirely out of class or, alternatively, it could be conducted as a class where you all go to the library together to find the texts and do the writing.

## Contributors

*David Gardner is senior language instructor in the English Centre of the University of Hong Kong. Lindsay Miller is assistant professor in the English Department at City University of Hong Kong.*

# Note-Taking Strategies—
# The Pyramid Method

**Levels**
Intermediate +

**Types**
English for academic
purposes

**Aims**
 Learn different ways of
note-taking

**Class Time**
45 minutes

**Preparation Time**
30 minutes to collect a
tape from a lecturer

**Resources**
None

For students preparing for academic study, good note-taking skills are essential. This is especially so for those working in a foreign language because the time pressure of listening and note-taking at the same time is often daunting. The technique used in this activity raises students' awareness of the range of strategies available for note-taking, enabling them to see the advantages and disadvantages of each and to choose those that suit them.

## Procedure

1. Have students listen to a lecture or a tape of an informative talk and take notes.
2. Pair off students and have them review each other's notes and make a list of good note-taking strategies and things to avoid. They can, of course, also take the opportunity to check their understanding of the content with each other.
3. Put the pairs into groups of four. Have each pair explain their list of strategies to the other pair, using the notes as examples. One student should be responsible for producing a combined list for the group.
4. Have the groups of four take turns presenting one of their strategies to the class. Write up a class list on the board. Continue until no new ideas are left. Encourage discussion as to why each strategy is or is not a good one.

## Caveats and Options

1. Produce as a handout a list of the class ideas for each student to keep.
2. Use this technique diagnostically to see which strategies the students are aware of. If there are significant gaps, fill them in during future lessons.

## Contributor

*Jo Hilder has taught ESL for several years at the English Language Institute, Victoria University of Wellington, in New Zealand, and is currently enrolled in the MA Program in TESL and Applied Linguistics at the University of California, Los Angeles.*

# Discovering Academic Writing Through Oral Skills

**Levels**
Advanced

**Types**
Academic writing
workshops for EFL
students in university
courses

**Aims**
Recognize academic
writing conventions for
editing own work
Build confidence in oral
presentation skills

**Class Time**
2 hours

**Preparation Time**
1 hour

**Resources**
Journal article
Handouts
Overhead transparencies

In this activity, students have a chance to read, write, and talk about a text from an academic journal. It draws on the skills and knowledge of the whole class.

## Procedure

1. Select a short journal article, for example from the *New Scientist*. Rewrite it using colloquial English. Be repetitious and use slang, phrasal verbs, and personal intrusions.
2. Divide the article into short paragraphs. Copy each paragraph so that all members of a group will have a copy of the paragraph assigned to their group. Use different colored paper for each paragraph. Copy each one onto an overhead transparency (OHT).
3. Introduce the activity by telling students they are going to act as editors for an academic publication. They have a submission with sound information but need to express it in a more acceptable form.
4. Divide the class into groups so that you have one group for each paragraph. Assign each group a paragraph, giving each individual in the group a copy of the paragraph to work on.
5. Allow class time for students to read their paragraphs individually and then discuss their paragraph with their group. Have them mark anything they think could be improved and suggest changes if possible.
6. Give out the relevant OHT to each group. Using their OHT, have each group (or a representative from each group) present their paragraph to the class, noting three comments and/or changes.
7. Encourage the class to discuss alternative structures, phrasing, and vocabulary with the presenters, writing examples on the whiteboard.

8. After group presentations, create a plenary discussion. Using whiteboard examples, elicit why the changes were made.
9. Create a *Look for* . . . list (see Appendix), that is, an academic writing checklist for editing their own work. Use examples from their texts and the whiteboard in the list.
10. Circulate the original article. Encourage students to notice their own improvements on the original.

## Caveats and Options

1. This activity allows a nonspecialist teacher in a field to use subject-based material.

## Appendix: Sample *Look for* . . . Checklist

Look for:
      repetition
      unnecessary words
      awkward, unclear phrasing
      phrasal verbs
      personal intrusions
      colloquial words/phrases

## Contributor

*Rosemary Lonsdale, senior academic coordinator of the English Language Unit, University of Wales, Aberystwyth, in the United Kingdom, is responsible for learning support and has taught English in the Middle East.*

# Using Video Sources for Academic Writing Practice

**Levels**
Advanced

**Types**
University tutorial

**Aims**
Write a critical review
Manipulate appropriate
evaluative language
Write using a common
critique structure
Generalize critique
writing to nonprint
media

**Class Time**
2 hours

**Preparation Time**
1 hour

**Resources**
Any short documentary
Worksheet
Model critique

This activity introduces students to the structure of a critical review through a model reading. The tutorial exercise, based on viewing a 25-minute documentary, requires students to write a critique having the same structure as the reading. This activity gives students practice applying critical concepts to nonprint sources and provides a way of teaching academic writing using visual stimuli as variation from the usual print-oriented teaching methods.

## Procedure

1. Review the structure of a critique (see Appendix).
2. Assign students to read an essay, such as Clegg & Wheeler (1991), that models the critique structure you want the students to practice. Discuss.
3. Explain to the students that the tutorial task will be centered around a short documentary. Students will be required to introduce, summarize, and evaluate the documentary.
4. Reinforce to the students that critics take different positions. These positions may be positive, negative, or mixed. Make sure that students understand that they will write profoundly different reviews because evaluation involves selecting particular points and making different judgments about the subject.
5. Have the students watch the video and take notes.
6. Ask students to summarize the main points of the documentary in small groups.
7. Have students discuss as a group what important points to select and what position to take.
8. Have students draft the critique.

## Caveats and Options

1. Make sure the video is no longer than 25 minutes.
2. Exchange the critiques and discuss differences between them.

# References and Further Reading

Arnaudet, M. L., & Barrett, M. E. (1984). *Approaches to academic reading and writing*. Englewood Cliffs, NJ: Prentice Hall.

Sollee, J. (1991). Jim Self's "lookout": Heed his warning! In C. S. Clegg & M. M. Wheeler (Eds.), *Students writing across the disciplines* (pp. 618-619). Fort Worth, TX: Holt, Rinehart & Winston.

## Appendix

1. Review the structure of the critique.
   Part I is the . . . What necessary parts should this paragraph contain?
   Part II is the . . . What goes in these paragraphs? Is the content subjective or objective?
   Part III is the . . . What do these paragraphs contain? Is the content subject or objective?
   Part IV is the . . . Is this part optional or essential?
2. Take notes in the space provided.
3. Write your critique. Label the different parts. Give your critique a title.

## Contributors

*Rose Lovell-Smith is a tutor for an English writing for academic purposes course open to native and nonnative fluent speakers of English at the University of Auckland, in New Zealand. Donna Starks is a lecturer for this course.*

# Genre, Discourse, and Academic Listening

*Levels*
High intermediate +

*Types*
University settings
Pre-university
preparation programs

*Aims*
Draw on discourse
structures as a
framework for listening
and note-taking in
academic settings

*Class Time*
1 hour

*Preparation Time*
30 minutes

*Resources*
Prepared listening
material
Note-taking grids

A knowledge of discourse structures can help students develop listening and note-taking skills in academic settings. This sample lesson shows how students can draw on their knowledge of particular discourse structures to listen and take notes in academic lectures. They then use these notes to write a text based on the same organizational patterns. The lesson thus simulates language use in academic settings where particular subject area content may be introduced within the context of one genre, the academic lecture, and then drawn on for the preparation of another genre, the academic essay.

## Procedure

1. Choose a short problem/solution text in a content area relevant to the students' present or future area(s) of study.
2. Take notes on the text under the categories of situation, problem/solution, and conclusion. Also take notes under the categories of reason and result within the problem component(s) of the text.
3. Use these notes to record a simulated version of an academic lecture.
4. Give the students the title of the lecture and the note-taking grid shown (see Appendix).
5. Ask students to predict the content of the lecture on the basis of the title and the discourse structure.
6. Play the simulated lecture to the students, telling them to listen to the lecture to confirm or correct their predictions.
7. Play the tape again, telling students to take more detailed notes under the situation, problem, solution, and conclusion headings given in the worksheet.

8. Play the tape once more, telling students to take notes under the reason and result headings in the worksheet.
9. Ask students to write a problem/solution text based on the notes they have taken from the simulated lecture.

## Caveats and Options

1. Not all lectures are based on problem/solution texts as this lesson might imply. Lectures may also be based on a number of other rhetorical patterns such as cause and effect, compare and contrast, description, and argument. Students should, in later lessons, be presented with tasks that focus on these organizational patterns as well.
2. Students can be asked to examine how the relationship between components of discourse structures, such as reason and result, is expressed grammatically. That is, they can be asked to identify connectives (e.g., *as a result*, *so*, and *therefore*), nouns (e.g., *cause*, *reason*, and *result*), verbs (e.g., *leads to* and *causes*) or groups of words that function like prepositions (e.g., *because of* and *due to*) and so on, depending on how the particular text has been presented.
3. Students can be asked to identify discourse structures that are not signaled linguistically but need to be inferred from the text. This is an extremely useful task for students to carry out as it is highlights the fact that the relationship between discourse structures is not always explicitly signaled in texts.

## References and Further Reading

Paltridge, B. (1995). Analyzing genre: A relational perspective. *System, 23*, 175-192.

# Appendix: Sample Note-Taking Grids

Title of lecture _____

| | |
|---|---|
| Situation | |
| Problem(s) | |
| Reason(s) | |
| Result(s) | |
| Solution(s) | |
| Conclusion(s) | |

# Contributor

*Brian Paltridge is senior lecturer in Applied Linguistics at the University of Melbourne in Australia. He has taught ESOL in Australia, New Zealand, and Italy.*

# Graph Reading

**Levels**
Advanced

**Types**
International English
Language Testing System
(IELTS) preparation

**Aims**
Progress from lower to
higher order skills in
graph reading

**Class Time**
1 hour

**Preparation Time**
Time needed to collect
and copy graphs

**Resources**
Graphs from various
subject areas

Reading and reporting on graphs calls on skills and knowledge in language as well as in content areas. Here students think, talk, and write about the topic of graphs.

## Procedure

1. Classify graphs into text types: pie charts, histograms, bar graphs, line graphs, and so on.
2. Discuss the type of information in each, referring to labels on the vertical and horizontal axes.
3. Have students speak and write sentences describing the information given in the graph (e.g., *In 1994 15% of all . . . were imported from . . .*).
4. Set higher order tasks such as comparing, inferring, and so on.

## Caveats and Options

1. If students have trouble understanding the graph's information, ask them to construct grammatically accurate sentences giving simple statements of the facts. This is particularly valuable when three or more variables are represented. It also usually demonstrates what kind of structure is most appropriate and leads to higher level tasks such as comparing and contrasting.
2. Be prepared for difficulties with pie charts or bar graphs when they show proportion or ratios. I find the structure *. . . account(s) for . . . % of the . . .* very useful for such figures.
3. Students can be given individual projects with a graph as a resource to be used as part of a short presentation to their classmates. The class

can then summarize the information. This is useful for a topic-based syllabus and gives practice in using library resources, finding statistics, and writing to local trade commissioners or consulate offices for facts and figures.

4. Useful sources of graphs are ESOL text-books like *Fluency squares*, *Panorama*, and the Nelson series Skills for Learning.

**References and Further Reading**

Knowles, P., & Sasaki, R. (1981). *Fluency squares for business and technology*. New York: Prentice Hall Regents.

Williams, R. (1982). *Panorama*. London: Longman.

## Contributor

*Craig Wallace has taught English in New Zealand, Australia, and the Middle East. He is currently director of studies for a language school in New South Wales, Australia.*

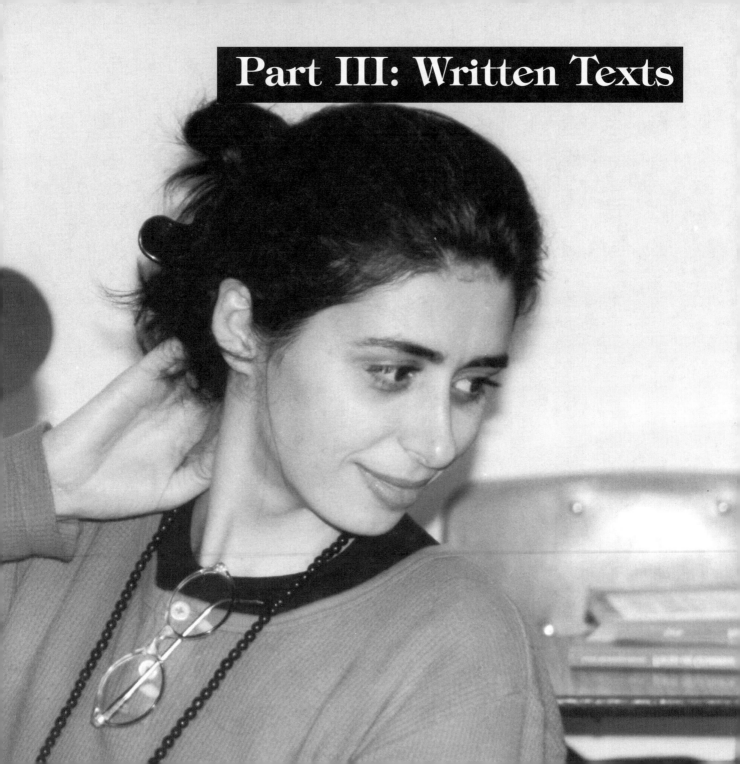

# Part III: Written Texts

*Sonia Lucas Mendonça at Northern Virginia Community College, Alexandria, Virginia USA.*

# Introduction

In this section, teachers suggest ways of starting lessons with some written text. Vocabulary learning is a common outcome for these lessons, but some use the written text as a jumping off point for developing skills in speaking and learning as well. One of the tasks suggests some physical as well as mental exercise. The sources of the texts are varied, too, including material written by the teachers themselves.

# Questioning the Text

**Levels**
Intermediate +

**Types**
Reading for academic purposes

**Aims**
Develop skills in critical reading of a text, especially in higher education

**Class Time**
One 90-minute class or two 45-minute classes

**Preparation Time**
30 minutes

**Resources**
Worksheet with nonsense text and questions
Information on question types and examples for discussion
Texts for resource material

Students can learn reading strategies that help them with particular, self-selected reading passages. These strategies also transfer to other contexts.

## Procedure

1. Give students a text that includes nonsense words substituted for many of the key information words, with two or three questions based on this text (see Appendix A). Have students read the text and attempt to answer the questions.
2. Ask some students for the answers they found to the questions and discuss briefly. Elicit the fact that students were able to give answers to the questions by including the nonsense words in their answers. Ask them, "Does this show understanding of the text?"
3. Present the students with a concise explanation of different types of questions, particularly higher/lower and open/closed (see Appendix B). Give a few examples and ask students what type of questions they are.
4. Pair off students and give each student a different text to read. These could be from one of their subject textbooks (if they are secondary or tertiary students who are studying other subjects) or from neutral texts if they are from very different disciplines. Tell them to make up questions based on the text so that they can test their partner on it.
5. After preparation time is finished, have students exchange resource sheets, read the text, and take turns testing each other on the content of the other's text.
6. To finish the lesson, hold a feedback session in which students reflect upon their performance as both questioner and questioned. Elicit ideas on the significance of this questioning for their own reading of texts.

## Caveats and Options

1. Instead of asking students to test each other in Step 5, you can ask them to read the text and guess what questions their partner is going to ask them. Discussion of the correlation between the questions made up and those anticipated can lead to interesting insights into the nature of the students' reading.
2. Various rules can be imposed upon the question types used. For example, you might tell students: "You can use a maximum of two questions to test factual knowledge" or "No question may have a yes/no answer or a purely factual answer."
3. You can tell the students to perform the main activity in groups of three or four, thus allowing for observers to judge the questions for type.
4. This could be compressed into one 45-minute lesson, with the loss of the awareness-raising activity and much of the discussion of question types.

## Appendix A: Sample Text and Questions

There are many ways to droffle a quadroid but the most infacious is the one imprined by the Drarkles of Sparcia. In this, the Drarkles—or empharcularly the young Drarkles—encand the spigglit of the quadroid to its fullest extand, then decand it rappingly, while sproggling it up and down astartly. This procedure can also be expunded to tridroids or pendroids.

Q1.  Who imprines the most infacious way to droffle a quadroid?
Q2.  Describe the process of droffling.
Q3.  Which Drarkles are most commonly identified with droffling?
Q4.  Is it only quadroids that can be droffled?

## Appendix B: Simplified Chart of Question Types

| O | C | Open or Closed question.<br>Relates to type of answer expected: C indicates a closed, or limited, set of answers. O indicates an open, or unlimited, set of answers. |
|---|---|---|
| H | L | Higher or Lower question.<br>Relates to type of thinking required: L normally indicates recall. |

Usually questions are open and higher order or closed and lower order, but an open question can involve lower order thinking, and a closed question can involve higher order thinking.

## References and Further Reading

Kissock, C., & Iyortsuun, P. (1982). *A guide to questioning*. London: Macmillan.

Lunzer, E., & Gardner, K. (1984). *Learning from the written word*. Edinburgh, Scotland: Oliver & Boyd.

Nuttall, C. (1982). *Teaching reading skills in a foreign language*. London: Heinemann.

Nunan, D. (1989). *Designing tasks for the communicative classroom*. Cambridge: Cambridge University Press.

## Contributors

*Rex Berridge, a teacher educator and formerly an English language adviser with the British Council, is now at the English Language Unit, University of Wales, Aberystwyth, in the United Kingdom. Jenny Muzambindo, a teacher educator and expert in English teaching and the methodology of teaching across the curriculum, is head of communication skills at Gweru Teachers' College, Zimbabwe.*

# The Emerging Markets Company

**Levels**
High intermediate

**Types**
University, private
language school,
secondary school

**Aims**
Skim and scan for
specific information
Discuss and synthesize
information

**Class Time**
40 minutes

**Preparation Time**
15 minutes

**Resources**
Copies of the data file

Students involved in this role play synthesize context that is real—which should lead to authentic language use among highly motivated students.

## Procedure

1. Ask students to discuss which countries in the world are regarded as developing countries, then give them a list of developing and developed countries (e.g., Germany, Mexico, Thailand, Britain, Malaysia, Nigeria, Korea, India, France, Brazil, Argentina, Italy, and Peru). Put students into groups and ask them to make two columns, Developed Countries and Developing Countries, and to place each country from the list in the appropriate column (see below).

| Developed Countries | Developing Countries |
|---|---|
| | |
| | |
| | |

3. After students distinguish countries that are developing from those that are developed, have them write the characteristics in another list.

| Developed Countries | Developing Countries |
|---|---|
| 1. | 1. |
| 2. | 2. |
| 3. | 3. |
| 4. | 4. |

4. Next, give students a handout with a list of countries in Column A and descriptions of countries in Column B (see Appendix A). Pair off students and have them match the countries in Column A to their corresponding descriptions in Column B.

5. Give students a list of criteria and ask them to rank the criteria from most to least crucial when choosing a country in which to invest (see Appendix B).

6. Give students the following list of countries (emerging markets) in which they can invest:

> Mexico, South Korea, Taiwan, Brazil, India, Malaysia, Thailand, Chile, Turkey, Argentina

Using the criteria in Step 5, tell them to find out as much as they can about these countries. If time is limited, give them information about each country (see Appendix C.) In groups have them decide on the percentage of their money to be invested in each country and give reasons for their choices (see sample chart below).

| Country | Percentage | Reason |
| --- | --- | --- |
|  |  |  |

## Appendix A: Matching Countries and Descriptions

| Countries | Description |
|---|---|
| Germany | It is located immediately south of the U.S. Its capital city is one of the most densely populated in the world. The people speak Spanish. Unemployment is just under 40%. The government has changed several times over the past decade. Its currency, the peso, is weak, though its supported by the dollar. Inflation is running at 50%. |
| Mexico | This country at one time was known as Siam. Situated in South East Asia, it has been poor for a long time. Recently, however, with low inflation and even lower interest rates, its exports are becoming very competitive. Its currency, the baht, is pegged to the U.S. dollar, giving it further security. |
| Thailand | In 1945, this country was in ruins. Today it is one of the strongest and most important countries in the world. Situated in central Europe, it dictates Europe's future. Its currency, the mark, is strong, while inflation is a mere 2%. |

## Appendix B: Investment Criteria

|  | population growth rate |
|---|---|
|  | low interest rates |
|  | low inflation |
|  | high exports |
|  | stable government |
|  | low unemployment |
|  | skilled labor force |

# Appendix C: Data File

### Latin America

Political instability has dominated the countries of this region for the past 2 years. It is even more important today with elections due in Mexico and the recent assassination of the Brazilian president.

The widespread discontent in Mexico is due in no small part to the corruption of the Salinas government. The rebellion of the Zapatistas rebels has added to the crumbling economy. The Mexican Finance Minister has raised interest rates to help its weak currency, the peso. Share prices are continuing to fall, but its economic history has been marked by periods of depression followed by sharp rises in the price of shares.

In the short term, Brazil looks very unstable, but with the new president, an economist by training, taking direct control of the economy the long term prospects are looking good. His recent decision to link the currency to the U.S. dollar has also given confidence to investors.

Argentina has devalued its currency, while Venezuela is suffering from the decrease in oil prices on which it is so dependent. Peru is regarded as having the worst prospects for the future based on its seemingly uncontrollable inflation and high interest rates.

### Asia

Because most currencies in this region are linked to the U.S. dollar, they naturally tend to respond to trends in the U.S. Thus, recent rises in interest rates have adversely affected investor confidence in markets such as those in Thailand and Malaysia. However, there seems to be political stability, and inflation is under control.

Chinese shares have done poorly. High interest rates and inflation and the recent death of Deng Xioping have caused shares to fall sharply. In the long term, gains are expected to be made.

Korea and Taiwan look like very impressive economies, but they are still young and growing. If you invest in them, you will be taking a great risk with the prospect of great gain.

Europe

The developing economies of Portugal, Greece, and Turkey all suffered from weak economies in 1993, 1994, and again in 1995.

Turkey has high inflation, but more importantly, it has huge national debts that have to be repaid to the World Bank.

Greece has changed considerably since it entered the EEC in 1992. However, trade unions have become stronger and regular strikes are having severe consequences for the economy.

Portugal seems to be a good investment, though things may change with the new socialist government.

**Contributor**

*Austin Conway has taught EFL in Europe and the Middle East in private language schools, secondary schools, and industrial training centers. He is now an instructor at Hong Kong University of Science and Technology.*

# The Running Dictation

**Levels**
Beginning–intermediate

**Types**
Any

**Aims**
Describe a person's
character
Develop accurate
writing, reading, and
listening skills

**Class Time**
30 minutes

**Preparation Time**
30–60 minutes

**Resources**
Poster with sentences
written on it

This activity combines a number of features. It can have new or familiar content; it integrates reading, speaking, listening, and writing; and finally, it keeps students physically active.

## Procedure

1. Make a poster with sentences describing a person's character (see Appendix). You may want to use vocabulary learned in previous lessons.
2. Have students work in pairs: One is the writer and the other is the runner. The runner must run to where the poster is (possibly in another room) and return to dictate the contents accurately. (Pairs may change roles half way through.)
3. When the pairs have recorded the sentences, have them rank the characteristics in order of what they see as the most important qualities in a person.
4. Put students into groups, and ask them to reach a consensus within their groups.
5. Compare group rankings as a whole class and, again, try to reach consensus.

## Caveats and Options

1. Instead of using sentences, you may choose a passage from a textbook or a story about what they did yesterday (e.g., *Yesterday I . . .*). Have students try to number the sentences in the correct sequence of events.

## Appendix: Sample Poster

A tolerant person is happy to listen to other people's ideas.
A sociable person loves being with other people.
An ambitious person . . .
A fussy person . . .
A reliable person . . .
A selfish person . . .
A moody person . . .
[other words describing character]

## Contributor

*Alison Gamble is currently a private ESL tutor. She studied at Auckland University and has a postgraduate diploma in ESL Teaching from the Australian Catholic University, in Melbourne, Australia.*

# Magazine Project

**Levels**
Intermediate

**Types**
Short-term university
courses in general
English

**Aims**
Improve basic language
skills in reading,
speaking, listening, and
writing

**Class Time**
5-6 hours +

**Preparation Time**
5 hours +

**Resources**
*Time* and *People Weekly*
magazines
Newsprint
Scissors, glue, white
paper, markers, scotch
tape
Handouts

## Procedure

1. Bring magazines to the classroom and give each student a copy. Briefly introduce the magazine(s), the content, the layout, the pictures, and so on. Explain the purpose of the project and assignments.
2. Tell the students to select one interesting article from the magazine and read about it. Ask them to take notes of the answers to five wh- and how questions and prepare an oral news report including personal reasons for choosing that article.
3. Ask the students to work in pairs or groups talking about the selected articles and then complete the Group Report chart followed by questions from other groups (see Appendix).
4. Now guide the students to write a news report in two or three paragraphs about the main idea of the article and reasons for their choice. Ask them to help each other with the first draft and then correct and revise their reports as homework.
5. Give each student a piece of white paper. Ask them to cut out the picture and glue it onto the upper part of the white paper and copy or glue their news report underneath.
6. Put up a class wallchart with all the completed magazine projects and take a class photo before publication.
7. Conduct a reflection period to discuss the learning experience.

## Caveats and Options

1. If you're working for an ESL program in the U.S., you can write to magazines such as *Time* and *People* about the possibility of receiving free copies.

## Appendix: Group Report Chart

| Article Name | Title | Who | When | Where | What | Why | How | Reasons for Choice |
|---|---|---|---|---|---|---|---|---|
|  |  |  |  |  |  |  |  |  |
|  |  |  |  |  |  |  |  |  |
|  |  |  |  |  |  |  |  |  |
|  |  |  |  |  |  |  |  |  |
|  |  |  |  |  |  |  |  |  |

## Contributor

*Peiya Gu teaches at Suzhou University in China. Previously she taught ESL to adult immigrants in New York while studying at Teachers College, Columbia University.*

# Using L1 to Teach L2

**Levels**
Intermediate +

**Types**
Students who share the same L1

**Aims**
Discover different cognitive processes available when using an L2

**Class Time**
30 minutes

**Preparation Time**
None

**Resources**
Any problem-solving activity (e.g., text reorganizing or reconstructing)
Visual or auditory stimuli (e.g., pictures or listening exercises)

I developed this idea for groups of students who spoke too much in English and Arabic, simultaneously causing confusion for both students and teacher, yet not enough in either Arabic or English separately to engage their minds creatively. The general insistence that students should use only their L2 in their L2 English class was proving counterproductive because it created interference that was actually inhibiting clear thinking in either language. I introduced an experimental methodology that encouraged students to evaluate which method—using Arabic or English—was more efficient for completing different kinds of problem solving tasks.

## Procedure

1. Select a problem-solving activity. Ask the students to divide themselves into two groups: those who always think and dream in L1 and those who sometimes think or dream in L2.
2. Require students to complete their L2 English task with their group using only the language they have selected.
3. Enforce the language selections as rigorously as possible (in a lighthearted, constructive way). For example, for the L1 group, allow students to use only a monolingual Arabic dictionary for this task, prohibiting them from saying any English words at all and even not allowing them to spell out words in English. Impose similar contrasting constraints for the L2 group. Both groups should be encouraged to speak loudly and volubly so that there is counterpoint between the two groups of speakers.
4. This will lead naturally to students evaluating the relative merits of the different approaches to using their L1 or L2. If a very clear analytical approach is taken here, the emphasis will be on the process

rather than on individual student performance, which can be forgotten in the activity. This focus on the activity rather than the individual makes the procedure particularly useful with mixed ability classes or with those classes where several students are more inhibited than others.

## Caveats and Options

1. Students may like to suggest their own parameters. For instance, some groups may communicate using facial expression only, while others might allow themselves to use body gesture only. Some individuals may decide that particular language activities might best be accomplished more efficiently standing up, while others may consider that they are more suitable for participants who are sitting down. An imaginative teacher or group of students can offer many more examples.

## Contributor

*Peter Hassall is International English Language Testing System (IELTS) administrator and examiner in the United Arab Emirates. He is the author of a number of ELT/EIL readers, study guides, and resource books. He is also the winner of three English Speaking Union prizes.*

# What Are the Differences?

**Levels**
Intermediate +

**Types**
English for social
sciences

**Aims**
Find out the differences
between a summary/
abstract and a letter of
transmittal as
preparation for the
writing of these two
documents

**Class Time**
1 hour

**Preparation Time**
30 minutes

**Resources**
Sample letter of
transmittal
Sample summary/
abstract
Envelope containing
strips of paragraphs cut
out from the samples
for each group

Students are often required to write a proposal together with its summary/abstract and a letter of transmittal as an assignment in a nonnative-speaking English for social science class. This activity is useful after the students have finished writing a proposal and are about to write the summary and the letter of transmittal. The group activity helps to teach the characteristics of a letter and a summary, saves time, and adds interest to the learning process.

## Procedure

1. Elicit from the students the components of a proposal (e.g., objectives, implementation plan, budget) as a lead-in to the students' search for content components in a sample letter and summary (see Appendices A and B).
2. Have students read the sample letter and summary, looking for the components.
3. Elicit the components of the letter and the summary and list them in a three-column chart on the chalkboard, following the order of the paragraphs in the samples (see Appendix C ).
4. Discuss the differences in content of the two pieces of writing in relation to their purpose and audience.
5. Put students into groups and give each group an envelope containing strips of mixed paragraphs cut out from the sample letter and summary.
6. Have each group put the paragraphs in the right order under the right type of writing. When students have trouble deciding whether a paragraph should go under a letter or a summary, ask them to look for the differences in format (e.g., sender's address, salutation, compli-

mentary close in the letter), language features (e.g., differences in use of pronouns and voice), and style (e.g., use of personal and objective tone) and their consistency within one type of writing. They can refer to the order of the components of the letter and chalkboard summary when they put the paragraphs in order under one type of writing. They should not be bothered by the content but should only focus their attention on the differences in format, language features, and style.

7. Elicit the differences that they have discovered in format, language features, and style of the letter and the summary and add the information onto the table on the chalkboard.
8. Go over the information on the table orally, giving a summary of the characteristics of a letter and a summary.
9. Have students write a letter of transmittal and a summary of their proposal following the guidelines that they have just worked out together on the chalkboard.

**Caveats and Options**

1. It is better for the students to have completed writing the draft of a proposal before this activity is carried out.
2. The same method can be applied to the teaching of English for other disciplines and in other contexts.

# Appendix A: Sample Letter

The Brilliant Youth Association
Room 323, Star Building
101, Oak Road
Kowloon

November 25, 1996

The Chairman
The Committee for the Promotion of Civic Education
Room 190, Central House
45, Central Road
Hong Kong

Dear Mr. Wong:

*Application for Funding of Project on Civic Education*

In response to your advertisement in the *Youth Post* on October 27, 1996 inviting applications for funding proposals, I am writing on behalf of the Brilliant Youth Association (BYA) to apply for funding of the Youth Courtesy Campaign.

The campaign is aimed at 8,000 teenagers aged 13–19 residing in West District, Hong Kong. A total of six events namely, slogan-design competition, cross-word puzzles competition, essay competition, an inter-estate quiz, an exhibition and an award ceremony, will be organized. The events will take place during the summer vacation from July 14, 1997 to August 30, 1997. In designing the programmes, we have considered the guidelines from your committee. We have enclosed a detailed programme proposal for your perusal.

We have chosen courtesy as our theme so as to remind young people about good manners. Courtesy is very important in promoting a good image of Hong Kong. Our community will also be more harmonious if people are courteous to one another. We have targeted young people since they are future masters of our society. As far as we know, this is the first time such a campaign has been carried out in Hong Kong.

With 30 years' experience in youth service, the Association is determined to serve the young people of Hong Kong. We can certainly get wide publicity for our programmes as we have well-established relationships with local and government organizations. We set a high standard for ourselves and will not disappoint you if given the opportunity.

We look forward to receiving your kind approval. If you require further information, please do not hesitate to contact us on 2339 4783.

Yours sincerely,

(Stephen Cheung)
Chairman

---

## Appendix B: Sample Summary/ Abstract

In response to the advertisement in the Youth Post on October 27, 1996 inviting applications for funding proposals, the Brilliant Youth Association is presenting its proposal entitled Youth Courtesy Campaign, which targets 8,000 teenagers aged 13–19 in the West District of Hong Kong.

The theme of courtesy has been chosen as it is important in promoting a good image of Hong Kong and can bring about harmony in society. Young people, who are future masters of society, are targeted.

During the summer vacation from July 14, 1997 to August 30, 1997, the following six events will be held in the Star Youth Center in West District:

1. slogan-design competition
2. cross-word puzzles competition
3. essay competition
4. an inter-estate quiz
5. an exhibition
6. an award ceremony

With 30 years' experience in youth service, the Association is determined to serve the young people of Hong Kong. Wide publicity can be secured for the programmes because of the Association's well-established relationships with local and government organizations. The campaign will be organized by the experienced staff of the Association on a budget of HK$20,000. To assess the effectiveness of the programmes, an evaluation report will be produced based on results of a survey and the participation records.

## Appendix C: Sample Chart

| Items for comparison | Letter | Summary |
|---|---|---|
| Content | 1. Introduction<br>2. Target population<br>Programmes<br>Date<br>3. Theme & rationale<br>4. Experience<br>5. Ending | 1. Introduction<br>( + target population)<br>2. Theme & rationale<br>3. Date & programmes<br>4. Experience<br>Budget<br>Evaluation |
| Format | Format of a letter | Format of an ordinary piece of writing |
| Language | Use personal pronouns (e.g., *I am writing* . . .)<br>Use active voice (e.g., *We have chosen courtesy as our theme* . . .) | Use the organization as the subject (e.g., The HKYA is presenting . . . ."<br>Use passive voice (e.g., *The theme of courtesy has been chosen* . . .) |
| Style | Personal tone<br>Persuasive (through word choice, e.g., *determined*) | Objective tone<br>Persuasive (through word choice, e.g., *secured*) |

## Contributor

*Belinda Ho is associate professor in the Department of English in City University of Hong Kong. She has taught ESL and EAP and is now teaching ESP.*

# Reformulating Student Texts

**Levels**
Advanced

**Types**
Undergraduate or
postgraduate writing
course
English for academic
purposes course

**Aims**
Analyze and improve
own texts

**Class Time**
30-50 minutes

**Preparation Time**
15-20 minutes

**Resources**
Students' texts or parts
of them typed up so as
to be anonymous
Teacher's or other
expert's rewriting of the
text

Giving students a focus when analyzing their own or their classmates' writing gives them the editorial job of evaluation and correction that the teacher is all too often expected to carry out. Having the students look at the teacher's suggestions for improvement in the reformulation only after they have made their own decisions helps students see the teacher's suggestions as just that.

## Procedure

1. Establish a sense of mutual trust in a class where writing is a focus. Start the process by encouraging students to share their writing and to exchange helpful comments for improvement where possible.

2. Ask students for permission to use their writing for a class activity in which they discuss small sections of each others' work, with a view to finding ways to improve the selection and ordering of information, as well as the language.

3. Take a representative text (i.e., one that illustrates problems that a number of people have been having) that the students have produced in response to a common writing task. Type it up just as it is and, on another sheet of paper or on the bottom part of the page, type a reformulated version that has been corrected and reorganized if necessary.

4. Ask the students to work first alone, then in pairs, and finally in groups to find the places in the student version of the text that they would want to improve. Ask each person to make suggestions for improvement and be prepared to give reasons.

5.  Next, have the students compare the teacher's reformulated version of the text to the suggestions that they have made and evaluate the teacher's suggestions.
6.  Ask the students to rewrite the text, or their own text, incorporating the suggestions they find useful.

## Caveats and Options

1.  Make sure that students are sensitive to each other's need for positive, constructive feedback.
2.  Vary the focus by choosing single sentences, paragraphs, or short whole texts to reformulate.
3.  Try to include texts from different students during the course.
4.  Ask students to reformulate a short text by themselves. Then use the student reformulations to brainstorm ways of improving a text.
5.  Generally speaking, this kind of feedback is only for those who have the metalanguage to discuss text.

## References and Further Reading

Cohen, A. D. (1989). Reformulation: A technique for providing advanced feedback in writing. *Guidelines, 11*, 1-9.

## Contributor

*Alison Hoffmann teaches in English for academic purposes and undergraduate second language writing programs at Victoria University of Wellington, New Zealand.*

# Question and Answer Quiz

**Levels**
Any

**Types**
English for reading

**Aims**
Interact with other
students in order to
negotiate language and
key concepts in texts
Scan and skim reading
of key concepts under
time constraints

**Class Time**
30-45 minutes

**Preparation Time**
5-10 minutes

**Resources**
Text that can sensibly
be divided into sections
and that extends
students' knowledge
about a familiar topic
Paper for each group

Students can be encouraged to see reading as an interactive process through an activity that practices questions.

## Procedure

1. Select a written text for the purposes of skimming and scanning. Divide the text into sections. Explain that the purpose of the activity is for each group to read and understand their particular section and to prepare three open and three closed questions based on important information.
2. Arrange individuals into groups. Ensure that each group is of mixed ability. Distribute a different section of the text to each group. Have students read individually or in pairs and then check their comprehension of the text by recalling key ideas with their group.
3. Have each group member write at least one question based on their understanding of key concepts. Group members check that they can answer and understand the form of all the questions.
4. Explain that while one group presents their questions to the class, the other groups must supply correct answers. The first group to answer accurately gets one point and the group with the most points wins.

## Caveats and Options

1. Instead of using a single text, use several short texts from different sources but on the same topic.
2. Students could be required to provide a few evaluative or application questions to encourage the use of background knowledge and greater engagement with content.
3. To save time, students could read the material out of class.

4. Tell each group that during the quiz they must take notes on the answers to the questions (key concepts) in each section. At the end of the question and answer session, each group must draw a diagram or chart of the key ideas contained within the full text. Groups compare charts.

## Contributor

*Angela Joe teaches at the English Language Institute, Victoria University of Wellington, in New Zealand, and has taught EFL in Japan. She is currently working toward a PhD in the area of vocabulary acquisition.*

# Have a Guess

**Levels**
Advanced

**Types**
Reading class for
student teachers
learning EFL

**Aims**
Practice strategies for
predicting the meaning
of new words in a text
Learn new vocabulary
Participate in an activity
that could be used later
with own students

**Class Time**
45 minutes

**Preparation Time**
15 minutes

**Resources**
Paragraph with some
words deleted

In some countries, teaching resources are at a minimum. This exercise requires nothing more than chalk and a blackboard.

## Procedure

1. Write up a paragraph with some words missing. Number the spaces.
2. Have the class read the passage aloud using numbers for the missing words.
3. Ask students to write down their guesses for the missing words individually.
4. Discuss the blanks one at a time, writing up all reasonable suggestions.
5. Supply the original word, emphasizing that most of their guesses are paraphrases or close synonyms that would have made sense and fit the context.
6. Ask which clues helped them to think of the missing words. Discuss linguistic and semantic contexts as clues for meaning.

## Caveats and Options

1. When no photocopier is available, the text needs to be short enough for the teacher to write on the board before the class arrives.

## Contributor

*Marilyn Lewis lectures on the Diploma and MA programs at the University of Auckland, in New Zealand. She sometimes runs workshops for foreign language teachers in other countries.*

# Ask Your Partner

**Levels**
Intermediate +

**Types**
Any

**Aims**
Formulate and use
questions to gather
information

**Class Time**
20–60 minutes

**Preparation Time**
20–30 minutes

**Resources**
Text of length
corresponding to
desired length of
activity

S tudents often have trouble forming questions in communicative situations. This activity is a way for them to gain skill in question formation by formulating questions which they then immediately use to gain information.

## Procedure

1. Divide the class into two equal-numbered groups. Give each member of Group 1 a copy of Handout 1 (see Appendix A), and each member of Group 2 a copy of Handout 2 (see Appendix B).
2. Have Group 1 read the passage under Part A in their handouts and discuss any uncertainties about meaning with each other. Have Group 2 work together to form questions according to the missing information in Part A of their handouts. As the groups work simultaneously, monitor and give assistance as needed.
3. When all students are prepared, have them pair off by finding a partner from the opposite group. Have the partners from Group 2 ask their questions and the partners from Group 1 answer according to the passage they have read.
4. When all pairs are finished, have students rejoin their original groups. Have the students repeat the exercise with Part B of the handouts, switching roles regarding questioning and answering.

## Caveats and Options

1. One text can be divided into two parts for the activity, so that Part B is a continuation of Part A, or two texts on related themes can be used.
2. This activity works very well with informational newspaper articles.
3. This activity can also be a useful prereading activity for a longer text, if done with an excerpt.
4. Student essays can also be used as text.

84

## Appendix A: Handout 1

A. Prepare questions to get the following information.

1. This passage is about (a person) _____.

   _____?

2. He was born in (a place) _____.

   _____?

3. True or false: He was educated in Sinhala medium. _____

   _____?

4. He went to England in order to _____.

   _____?

5. In 1953 he became _____.

   _____?

6. He introduced _____.

   _____?

7. True or false: He was able to finish Ratmalana Airport. _____

   _____?

B. Read the following passage and prepare to answer your partner's questions on it.

In addition to his political and civic accomplishments, Sir John Kotalawela was successful in his military career. From the rank of Commissioned Officer which he attained in 1922, he progressed to General of the Sri

Lankan Volunteer Force. His dedication to the betterment of Sri Lanka's military led to his donating a large piece of land, known as Kandawela Estate, to the government for the establishment of a National Defense Academy.

Sir John Kotalawela died on October 2, 1980. Today he is known as a national hero of Sri Lanka.

**Appendix B: Handout 2**

A. Read the following passage and prepare to answer your partner's questions on it.

Sir John Kotalawela was born in Ceylon, as Sri Lanka was called at the time of his birth. Following his education in an English-medium missionary school, he went to England to pursue his higher studies. After his return, he undertook dual careers in politics and in the military. He was to make great achievements in both of these fields.

Sir John was a member of the first State Council established by the British on June 13, 1931; and on October 12, 1953, he became Prime Minister of Ceylon. The great contributions he made during his political career include the construction of the Peradeniya University campus, the introduction of civil aviation and the completion of Ratmalana Airport. He is also known for his efforts to achieve the entry of Ceylon into the United Nations.

B. Prepare questions to get the following information.

1. In 1922 Sir John became _____ .

_____ ?

2. True or false: He advanced in his military career. _____

_____ ?

3. Later he became General of _____ .

_____ ?

4. He made a gift of some land to _____.

_____?

5. He donated the property for (a purpose) _____.

_____?

6. He died on (a date) _____.

_____?

## Contributor

*Theresa McGarry is a Peace Corps volunteer teaching at Rahangala Affiliated University College in Boralanda, Sri Lanka. Previously she taught in Japan and Korea.*

# Take Your Vorpal Sword in Hand and Write

**Levels**
Intermediate +

**Types**
Any

**Aims**
Improve reading skills
Develop awareness of
grammatical accuracy in
writing
Write creatively and
imaginatively
Practice oral
communication skills

**Class Time**
1 hour

**Preparation Time**
None

**Resources**
One copy of a short
nonsense story or poem
for each student

This activity gives students a chance to practice their reading, writing, and speaking skills in an enjoyable way, using what looks at first to be a meaningless text.

## Procedure

1. Give each student a copy of the text and enough time to read the text once.
2. Have students re-read the text and list 10 words that are unfamiliar to them.
3. Next to each unknown vocabulary item, ask them to write down what part of speech it is and what they think it might mean.
4. Go over the text with the students, writing their list of unknown words on the board. Work together and decide upon the parts of speech and meanings. Write the part of speech next to each word. Leave the meanings of the nonsense words to students' judgment.
5. When you are satisfied they have come to an understanding of the text (not necessarily resembling your own), discuss with them whether they found it useful to look at what part of speech the word is in trying to understand its meaning. Also discuss the presence of sense in a piece of nonsense writing.
6. Have students write their own short nonsense text (poem or story), which should make some sense to the reader. They can use vocabulary from the text you have given them or make up their own nonsense words. Allow them 10 minutes only, as they are not to elaborate.
7. Have students exchange their writing with a student sitting in a different part of the room. Have them read each other's texts, listing the unknown words with their part of speech and likely meaning.

8. Ask partners to move and sit together to negotiate the intended and the derived meanings.

## Caveats and Options

1. At the end of the activity, you may choose to collect the writings, as they will provide you with an insight into your students' creative talents, as well as their ability to handle grammatical structure and vocabulary.
2. A poem that works very well is Lewis Carroll's "Jabberwocky," which you can find in almost any anthology of English literature.
3. Ask students to draw a picture of an imaginary object mentioned in the text, for example, the Jubjub bird in "Jabberwocky" (or the Tumtum tree, or better still, the Jabberwock) as they imagine it to be. When they finish, show them (or give them a copy of) a sketch of a bird (or tree, or Jabberwock) of your own. Then ask them to compare their own drawings with your sketches. Go over useful language items for comparison (e.g., *more than, similarly*).

## References and Further Reading

Carroll, L. (1986). *Jabberwocky*. In M. H. Abrams (Ed.), *The Norton anthology of English literature* (5th ed., vol. 2, pp. 1594–1595). New York: Norton. (Original work published 1871)

# Contributors

*Wisam Mansour is assistant professor of English at the Applied Science University in Amman, Jordan. Selda Mansour has a BA in ELT and previously taught EAP. At present she is rearing a trilingual child.*

# Retelling With a Difference

**Levels**
Intermediate +

**Types**
General English courses
with emphasis on
speaking and listening

**Aims**
Gain knowledge of a
particular topic while
improving speaking and
listening skills
Learn new vocabulary in
context

**Class Time**
50 minutes

**Preparation Time**
30 minutes

**Resources**
Two articles on the
particular topic or
subject being taught
Quiz questions based on
the articles

Here is an idea that can be adapted to practically any text chosen by the teacher or by the students.

## Procedure

1. Divide the class into two groups, each group on one side of the room.
2. Explain the rules:
   - Each group is to read an article and then tell the main points to the other group.
   - Speakers must make sure that the listeners understand them.
   - There will be a quiz at the end to check which group is the best in retelling.
   - They have 15 minutes to read. They can ask for meaning and pronunciation of new or difficult words.
3. Distribute the articles. Give each group one article. Note the time, then tell students to start reading.
4. Circulate around the room to answer queries and to check students' ability to accomplish the task within the given time. Give more time if necessary.
5. Count down the last 3 minutes silently by writing the remaining number of minutes on the board one by one (i.e., 3, 2, 1).
6. Have students pair off with a student from the other group.
7. Give them 10 minutes each to tell the other about what they read. Have each pair work out who goes first.
8. Repeat Steps 4 and 5.
9. Stop students and have them change partners.
10. Repeat Steps 4 and 5.
11. Have students return to their groups.

12. Ask each group five questions on what they have heard from the other group. Give each correct answer one point.
13. Add up the scores and announce the winner.

## Caveats and Options

1. It is important to choose articles that are at a slightly lower level than the students' English level to ensure enjoyment and success.
2. The time allowed for reading and retelling tasks can be lengthened or shortened to vary the degree of difficulty to suit students.

## Contributor

*Trinh Thi Sao teaches in the School of Languages at Auckland Institute of Technology, New Zealand. She has taught ESL and Vietnamese.*

# Small-Group Activities

**Levels**
Advanced

**Types**
Small-group activities for
university students

**Aims**
Gain more opportunity
for individual attention
to skill development
within large classes

**Class Time**
50 minutes +

**Preparation Time**
2–3 hours to organize
groups and materials
1–2 hours to train
assistant teachers

**Resources**
Reading materials and
writing topics for
students
Teaching materials for
graduate assistants
working as assistant
teachers

When teachers are faced with large classes, one solution is to include native speakers as language sources and small-group facilitators. With some guidance, as suggested here, graduate assistants can encourage small-group interaction.

## Procedure

1. Work with the graduate students you have selected to be assistant teachers. Offer them methodology books and other materials on teaching reading and writing in small groups. Train them also in small-group interaction.
2. Organize groups of four to five students by general ability. Assign each group an assistant teacher.
3. Provide as much class time as possible for the groups.
4. Use some large-group instruction for general information and feedback.
5. Use half of the semester for reading improvement with authentic materials.
6. Use half of the semester for process writing: prewriting, draft writing, editing, evaluating, final drafts, and possible publication.

## Caveats and Options

1. Be flexible in switching students and teachers if desired.
2. Be flexible organizing time spent in groups.
3. The success of this activity depends upon the availability of graduate student/assistant teachers.

## References and Further Reading

Aaron, J. E. (1990). *The compact reader.* Boston: St. Martin's Press.

Watkins-Goffman, L., & Berkowitz, D. (1990). *Thinking to write.* New York: Maxwell Macmillan International.

## Contributor

*Arlene Schrade teaches EFL and directs the MA and PhD programs in TESOL at the University of Mississippi, in the United States. She received her PhD in Foreign Language Education at the Ohio State University and has been a teacher of English and Spanish and a teacher trainer for many years.*

# Shared Dictation Game

**Levels**
Any

**Types**
Reading class

**Aims**
Remember short
phrases and
communicate these
accurately

**Class Time**
20 minutes

**Preparation Time**
10 minutes

**Resources**
Several copies of a
short, high interest text
(e.g., a poem, a
paragraph from a story,
a travel brochure, or an
ESP text)
Adhesive

This activity is an enjoyable way to break the ice in a new ESOL classroom as it encourages pair work, focuses on clarity in pronunciation, and helps short-term retention of phrases, clauses, and sentences. It also encourages students to speak in a nonthreatening situation where the emphasis is on conveying written information accurately so that it may be written up in the same form.

## Procedure

1. Prepare the text in advance. Make several copies of the text and number them. Put up the texts in the corridor outside the classroom with adhesive.
2. Pair off students, designating one person as A and the other as B.
3. Give each pair a number.
4. Ask A to sit while B runs out, looks at their numbered text, and memorizes a chunk. Have B run back and dictate the chunk to A, who writes it down. B then runs out to get the next chunk.
5. When the whole text has been reproduced, have both partners compare their copied text to the original version.

## Caveats and Options

1. This is a good activity to use in a language through literature classroom with poems, prose poems, and short prose pieces.
2. Competition can be built into the game so that the pairs compete to complete the relayed copying of the text.

3. The game may also be played in groups with one person running out, memorizing chunks, and then repeating it to a group of learners who write it down. Learners compare their texts with each other at the end.

## Contributor

*Nikhat Shameem is a lecturer in the Institute of Language Teaching and Learning at the University of Auckland, in New Zealand.*

# Part IV: Direct Teaching

*Majed Jamal at Northern Virginia Community College, Alexandria, Virginia USA.*

# Introduction

This section of the book includes activities that call for direct teaching as their starting point. The range of ideas shows that direct teaching as one part of a lesson need not be boring and can lead to a range of learning outcomes for the students.

# Holiday Speeches

**Levels**
Any

**Types**
Any, with a variety of
cultures represented

**Aims**
Develop sense of
community with other
students
Exchange meaningful
information on culture
Give and listen to
speeches

**Class Time**
5–10 minutes per
student

**Preparation Time**
5–10 minutes per
student for checking
drafts

**Resources**
Handout

Holidays are a good topic for students to speak about because all students have experienced them, and the speeches can be personal or academic as students prefer. In ethnically diverse classrooms, students enjoy teaching and learning about the holidays of other cultures.

## Procedure

1. Tell students to choose a holiday that they celebrate or observe in their country of origin. They will be responsible for writing a short speech telling other class members about that holiday. They should include such things as the history of the holiday, traditional food, symbols, costumes, and customs. Encourage students to be creative and to include sensory descriptions of the holidays. What is the atmosphere like? What are the smells, the sounds, and the feelings? Students should bring in photographs and other aids.

2. Present a lesson on what makes a good speech. Elicit from students elements such as use of clear statements and structures, eye contact, audience participation, and visual aids.

3. Give students a day or two to choose a holiday and to turn in a worksheet with the basics of the speech (see Appendix). Then give them 2 more days to turn in a draft of the speech.

4. Read each paper and make sure the ideas are clear enough for the class. Note if there are any unclear ideas or if you have questions. Hand back the papers, answer any questions students have about your comments, and give them a few days to revise.

5. Give each student 3–5 minutes to deliver their presentation. Tell them to time themselves while practicing at home and enlist a friendly timekeeper who can flash *1 minute left* and *time's up* cards as

speakers reach the end of 5 minutes. Encourage the audience to ask questions at the end of the speeches. Two or three speeches can be given at the end of class each day for several days to avoid monotony or overload.

## Caveats and Options

1. A short quiz or some other form of check or review can be given based on the information in the speeches.
2. If several distinct cultures are represented in the class, they could make groups and spend a few minutes brainstorming or talking about various holidays, even in their L1, to activate memories and ideas prior to choosing a holiday.

## Appendix: Holiday Sharing

*Directions:* Fill in the information for any of the categories which apply to the holiday you have chosen.

Holiday name:

History:

Special food and drinks:

Special costumes:

Symbols and their meanings:

Customs:

Feelings and thoughts associated with this holiday:

Other (for example, your family's traditions) :

## Contributor

*Elizabeth Bigler taught English in Japan for 3 years and has taught ESL in Atlanta, Georgia, in academic, adult, and refugee programs. Her MA in Applied Linguistics/ESL is from Georgia State University, in the United States.*

# Time Lines

**Levels**
Intermediate +

**Types**
Any students having
difficulty with time
referencing concepts

**Aims**
Reinforce tense and
aspect concepts and
practice differentiating
between them

**Class Time**
45 minutes

**Preparation Time**
10–15 minutes

**Resources**
Worksheet

With a renewed interest in including grammar in communicative language classes, teachers are looking for activities that go beyond traditional exercises. The sentences in this activity can be adapted to suit the class's interests.

## Procedure

1. If necessary, review tense and aspect concepts (e.g., simple past, past continuous, conditionals, present-as-future).
2. Make sure students know what to do with a time line. The accepted convention is a cross (x) for a point of time, and a wavy line (~) for continuous time.
3. Hand out the worksheets (see Appendix) and get students to fill them in, preferably in pairs or small groups.
4. When most have finished, have students put their answers on the board. Discuss any errors or alternatives.

## Caveats and Options

1. A useful follow-up activity to practice these concepts further in a communicative way is to prepare a "Find someone who" sheet using as many of the tense/aspect constructions as possible.

## Appendix: Sample Worksheet for Expressing Time in English

*Directions:* Put these verbs in the appropriate places on the time lines. For example:

yesterday

↗

I went to town yesterday.     P _____ x _____ N _____ F

I was in town when it rained.     P ~~~~~x~~~~~ N _____ F

↗

rain

I love *Hamlet*.                                          _____

I am reading *Hamlet*.                                _____

I read *Hamlet*.                                          _____

I have finished *Hamlet*.                          _____

I have been reading *Hamlet*.                  _____

I was reading when the phone rang.        _____

I had read *Hamlet* before I saw the film.   _____

I am going to read *Hamlet*.                      _____

I used to read a lot.                                    _____

I am about to start reading *Hamlet*.         _____

I leave tomorrow.                                       _____

If I won Lotto, I would buy a new car.        _____

The plane leaves at 6:00 p.m.                              _____

Auckland's weather is changeable.                          _____

He would phone me every day.                               _____

President Clinton meets the
    Prime Minister soon.                                 _____

I wondered if I could see you now.                         _____

The Rolling Stones have asked for quiet.                   _____

When he arrives, I will have finished.                     _____

## Contributor

   *Carol Griffiths is senior tutor at a language institute in Auckland, New Zealand. She is currently studying for an MA in Applied Linguistics and plans to start a doctorate. Previously, she taught high school.*

# Teacher as Postman

**Levels**
Beginning +

**Types**
ESOL

**Aims**
Practice letter writing in
a meaningful context
Establish contact with
other learners in a
similar situation

**Class Time**
30 minutes

**Preparation Time**
None

**Resources**
None

An alternative to writing to the teacher is to establish links between her students and students from another class. Where the institute has different classes at the same level, it is a good idea to have these students write to each other. Their letters may be purely factual but often the correspondence soon develops into a discussion of common concerns about both language and immigrant issues. Students writing to peers at the same level are less concerned about making a good impression (e.g., when a beginning-level student writes to an advanced student or a student writes to a teacher) and more concerned with getting meaning across and exploring common problems. The benefit is both linguistic and personal.

## Procedure

1. Introduce or review letter writing conventions.
2. Explain that students are going to write to fellow students in a parallel class.
3. Collect letters and write brief notes to the teacher of the parallel class to ensure that age is taken into consideration and that students write to someone from a different language background wherever possible.
4. After the first letter, students will be able to address their penpals by name and the teacher will simply act as postman.

## Caveats and Options

1. For the first letter with a beginning-level group, students can be encouraged to use work from class topics (e.g., daily routines).
2. Students soon develop their own personal style and should be encouraged to do so. For example, one student put all her letters in an

envelope decorated with her own drawings and another checked language use with me before writing.

3. A Meet Your Penpal party can be planned (possibly organized through the letters) for the end of the semester to motivate students to maintain the correspondence.

## Contributor

*Alison Kirkness is a teacher of ESOL and a teacher educator who works at the Auckland Institute of Technology in New Zealand. She has also taught EFL in Germany.*

# Exploiting the
# Answering Machine

**Levels**
Beginning

**Types**
General ESOL

**Aims**
Speak on the phone
with greater confidence

**Class Time**
5 minutes

**Preparation Time**
None

**Resources**
Answering machine for
the teacher
Access to a phone for
each student

Leaving a message on an answering machine can be a daunting experience for beginning-level students. They can be encouraged to practice and gain confidence by leaving messages for the teacher on her answering machine regularly. The messages should be real (e.g., a piece of information they have had to look up for homework or arrangements for a class outing)—the more realistic the better.

## Procedure

1. Practice telephone conventions with the class.
2. Distribute lists of class names and have the students exchange phone numbers. They should be encouraged to keep in touch with each other by phone to clarify homework, explain absence, and so on.
3. Introduce the idea of a class outing.
4. Assign responsibilities to each person, for example:
   - find out bus timetable or students who can help with car transport
   - find out opening hours, entry fee for place to be visited
   - list things to be taken for the day
   - organize a wet weather alternative
   - organize food and drink
   - organize meeting time and place
5. Make it clear that you need all the information and that students must leave it on your answering machine.

## Caveats and Options

1. Say you want to check phone numbers and the list is at home. Invite students to ring you at home with the information and leave it on the answering machine.

## Contributor

*Alison Kirkness is a teacher of ESOL and a teacher educator who works at the Auckland Institute of Technology, in New Zealand. She has also taught EFL in Germany.*

# Literacy Lines

**Levels**
Beginning

**Types**
Revolving admissions in
a public education adult
literacy setting

**Aims**
Learn sight words along
with the alphabet

**Class Time**
45–50 minutes

**Preparation Time**
30–60 minutes

**Resources**
Computer with a
graphics font (e.g.,
*Cairo*) or another
source of pictures

Prebeginning or preliterate learners present a challenge to the ESL teacher accustomed to students who can write the Latin alphabet. This activity presents a way to develop sight skill exercises without delaying communicative functions. The technique utilizes whole word recognition in a mixed holistic approach that involves all the skills of language, not just the recitation of the alphabet. Students approach the script on both a whole word (or sight word) and a phonological level. The two subskills of phonetic decoding and sight word recognition work together, and learners should be encouraged to apply both strategies.

## Procedure

1. Approach the writing and reading problem on two fronts. The alphabet can be taught along with sight words that are in daily use in the classroom (see Appendix A).
2. As the class is working on the sight words and conversation skills necessary for pre-beginners, introduce the four literacy subskills of visual discrimination, visual memory, visual sequencing, and active vocabulary. Choose words that are already in active use even if they are not on the official vocabulary list. While practicing the words, the learners begin to associate the symbols with the sounds, and they begin to recognize familiar words in different contexts. For example, they may learn *stop* in an exercise on traffic signs and then see the word again in an advertisement, (e.g., *Stop smoking now*) or they may meet the word on an exam.
3. In the set of sample exercises (see Appendix B) students recognize common words and the more advanced fill in the missing letters or even write out the whole words. Students remember the visual images of these sight words along with the phonetic equivalents. At

the same time, basic beginners work on the alphabet. The sight words give students something to work with right away while they are learning how to decode them phonetically.

## Caveats and Options

1. This exercise should contain meaningful words that are in daily use.
2. Additional exercises can be constructed to help in the literacy subskills of visual discrimination, left-right orientation, and sound-symbol correspondence, for example:

   Mark the number that is different:

   | 1 | 1 | 2 | 1 |
   |---|---|---|---|
   | 4 | 3 | 3 | 3 |
   | 6 | 9 | 6 | 6 |

3. You should always review previous material.

## References and Further Reading

Bowen, J. D., Madsen H., & Hilferty, A. (1985). *TESOL techniques and procedures.* Rowley, MA: Newbury House.

Krashen, S. D., & Terrell, T. D. (1983). *The natural approach.* Oxford: Pergamon.

## Appendix A: Sight Words

A. Forms

Name  _____

Address  _____

Social Security Number  _____

Telephone Number  _____

**Appendix B: The Alphabet**

B. Signs

| | | | |
|---|---|---|---|
| Men | ♂ | Post Office | ✉ |
| Women | ♀ | Exit | **EXIT** |
| Stop | **STOP** | Wet Paint | 🪣 |
| Railroad Crossing | ⊗ | | |

C. Warnings

| | | | |
|---|---|---|---|
| Danger | **DANGER** | Caution | **CAUTION** |
| Poison | ☠ | | |

Copy:

A B C D E F G H I J K L M N O P Q R S T U V W X Y Z

A _ _ _ _ _ _ _ _ _ _ _ _ _ _ _ _ _ _ _ _ _ _ _ _ _

a b c d e f g h i j k l m n o p q r s t u v w x y z

a _ _ _ _ _ _ _ _ _ _ _ _ _ _ _ _ _ _ _ _ _ _ _ _ _

Complete the Words:

1. Frog

   Fr<u>og</u>

2. Egg

   _gg

3. Hand

   H_nd

4. The moon

   The moo_

5. Star

   S_ar

6. Pencil

   _encil

7. Chair

   Cha_r

**Contributor**

*Douglas Magrath teaches ESL at Seminole Community College and Embry-Riddle Aeronautical University, in the United States. He also trains teachers for Lake County, Florida.*

# What Do I Write Next?

**Levels**
Intermediate

**Types**
Writing lesson for
university foreign
language students

**Aims**
Learn several ways of
expanding a topic
sentence
Review cohesive devices
in writing

**Class Time**
45 minutes

**Preparation Time**
5 minutes

**Resources**
Chalkboard

For some students, the greatest difficulty in writing in a new language is finding the ideas. Showing them how to build on key ideas is one way to overcome the block.

## Procedure

1. Ask students about difficulties they have had in expanding a list of topic sentences into paragraphs.
2. Agree on a topic of interest.
3. On one side of the board, write a topic sentence for paragraph 1, preferably a sentence suggested by the students (e.g., *People are interested in beautifying our town.*).
4. Elicit from the class a number of key ideas that could follow—reasons, methods, obstacles, and results.
5. Elicit examples of each. List these on the other side of the board.
6. Try linking some of these with the first sentence, using various cohesive devices (e.g., *One way of doing this would be . . . .*).
7. Have students write one paragraph each, using the same topic sentence and drawing on the ideas on the board.

## Contributors

*This activity was developed by Marilyn Lewis with other teachers of English and one of their classes at the Qui Nhon Teachers' College, Vietnam.*

# Listening, Responding, Self-Evaluating

**Levels**
Intermediate +

**Types**
Conversation class

**Aims**
Gain self-confidence in speaking and listening

**Class Time**
1 hour

**Preparation Time**
30 minutes

**Resources**
Self-evaluation sheet

In this activity, students are asked to choose topics that they are interested in (e.g., friends, clubs, family, favorite vacations, sports, pets, favorite parks, giving a demonstration, explaining a process). Vocabulary learned is practical, everyday, conversational vocabulary for familiar concepts. The self-evaluation component provides motivation for students to improve their listening and speaking skills. If students can evaluate themselves, they can progress at their own pace and take responsibility for their own learning.

## Procedure

1. For the first few days of class, have the students introduce themselves and get to know one another using English or their L1.
2. After a few days, teach and practice a brief introduction, such as:

   Hello, my name is Yuko (introduction). I live in Musashi-Sakai. There are four people in my family. My mother, my father, my younger sister and me. We also have a cat named Tobby (presentation). Thank you (conclusion).

3. Ask students to bring pictures of their family to school as props to introduce their families to their classmates, at first in small groups and then to the whole class. Teach the meaning of the words *volunteer, active listening*, and *courteous* before students make the introductions. Encourage them to applaud each other's achievements after each speaker concludes the presentation by saying *thank you*.
4. Next, teach the meaning of *comment* and *question*. Have them give their presentations again. Listeners should be courteous, listen carefully, and be prepared to ask a question or make a comment to the speaker. Questions and comments by the listeners, in the beginning,

will usually be closed-ended such as, *Is your mother a housewife?* or, *I like cats too.* In the beginning, speakers should be allowed to write down and read what they want to say. Later, however, they should be encouraged to use note cards for presentations.

5.  Introduce the phrases *participation* and *English only.* After students understand the meaning of these new phrases, teach the self-evaluation process. The self-evaluation process is based on 100 possible points that can be earned in six categories (see Appendix).

6.  Let the class know the grading scale and equate it with the words *excellent, above average*, and so on.

7.  At the beginning of each class, have students write their names on a piece of paper along with the category list. During the class, ask them to keep track of their own points. Make it clear from the beginning that active listening is one of the main focuses of the lesson. If students raise their hands to ask a question or make a comment, they earn points. Question and comment points are earned only by the listeners.

8.  For the third time, let students introduce their families and let them try out the self-evaluation process. (By this time, students should be more comfortable with the new vocabulary and one another.) Monitor students to make sure they understand the process and do not over- or undercalculate. At the end of the class, have students hand in their self-evaluation papers for recording. Return the evaluations at the next class meeting so students can monitor their progress. At the end of the semester add up and average the points. Delete the two or three lowest scores from all student lists as it takes time for students to understand what is expected of them.

9.  Practice using the self-evaluation format. Again, have students choose any subject to talk about. Inform them that small photographs from home do not work well from the front of a large classroom. Students can also bring other props from home like CDs, posters, or even baseball gloves or other sports equipment. At this phase, the goal is to move to open-ended dialogue. That is, students should begin to respond with more than yes or no.

## Caveats and Options

1. If the instructor wishes to use this process as a writing exercise, presentations can be written out and evaluated according to whatever writing patterns the instructor is working on (e.g., opening paragraph, body and conclusion, parts of speech, tense, sentence structure, mechanics).

## Appendix: Self-Evaluation

| Category List | Points |
|---|---|
| 1. active listening | 1 to 10 possible points |
| 2. active participation | 1 to 10 possible points |
| 3. being courteous | 1 to 10 possible points |
| 4. volunteering | 1 to 10 possible points (e.g., hand raising) |
| 5. English only | 1 to 10 possible points |
| 6. questions/comments | 10 points each—50 points maximum |

100 points possible (earned only by listeners)

## Contributor

*Larry J. Sinnott teaches at the English Language Education Research Institute, Asia University, Tokyo, Japan.*

# Vocational Literacy for Rural Community Development

**Levels**
Beginning

**Types**
Vocational literacy
classes

**Aims**
Acquire literacy skills in
the context of income-
generating activity and
social reconstruction

**Class Time**
2 hours

**Preparation Time**
1 hour

**Resources**
Context-appropriate
literacy courses (L1 and
L2)
Vocational modules
geared to selected
lessons from the literacy
courses, in line with
nationally approved
Adult Basic Education
(ABE) levels and
competencies

Existing published Adult Basic Education (ABE) materials are used in conjunction with vocation-specific modules and, where appropriate, homemade training videos. The vocation-specific modules (e.g., literacy for sewing, for leathercraft, for small business development) are developed and written in response to needs articulated by specific Community Learning Centers.

In deep rural contexts, adequate social motivation for the acquisition of literacy skills is often lacking. By teaching literacy as an integral part of community reconstruction and focusing on the development of specific income-generating activities, learners can begin to see literacy as one important way of taking charge of their lives and communities.

## Procedure

1. Put students into small groups according to ability and level. While you work with the first group, have the other groups practice what they learned in the previous lesson.
2. For each group, outline the task to be learned (e.g., using an invoice book, selecting leather for soles and uppers, or threading a sewing machine). Take care to explain the place of this task in the module as a whole and how long the task should take.
3. Demonstrate the task to the group. Prompt learners to respond verbally during the demonstration (e.g., by drawing on their background experience, eliciting advice, or asking questions).
4. Ask the learners to perform the task, guided by you or by a very competent learner. Once assured that learners are progressing satisfactorily, move on to the next group. Ask the students to continue practicing the task on their own, as a group, discussing each step with each other, and correcting each other's performances.

5. In the second part of the lesson, ask learners to work in their groups with the appropriate vocational literacy materials (e.g., task sheets, workbooks) that relate directly to the language (vocabulary, discourse structures, specific terminology) acquired in the task just performed. These materials exercise the newly acquired language competencies by means of reading, writing, and discussion activities.

6. If possible, provide opportunities at the end of the lesson for individual learners (perhaps shy or less confident people) to perform the task on their own. Be available to assist if needed.

## Caveats and Options

1. Having ascertained the community's own assessment of a realistic best hope option for creating sustainable economic activity, it is useful to cooperate with other ABE agencies to obtain an independent assessment of its economic and logistical viability in context.

2. Allow learner groups to proceed at their own pace.

## Contributor

*Laurence Wright is director of the Institute for the Study of English in Africa, at Rhodes University, in South Africa.*

# Part V: Worksheets to Complete

*Edgard H. Delgado, Hoang Mai Kim, and Javier Obradovich at Northern Virginia Community College, Alexandria, Virginia USA.*

# Introduction

Since the arrival of the photocopier, teachers have found many ways of livening up their lesson materials, as the examples in this section show. On the other hand, teachers who find themselves without photocopiers can often adapt the same ideas by using the chalkboard or by making their own material by hand and then sharing the materials with other teachers to make the effort worthwhile.

# Idiom Bingo

**Levels**
Beginning-intermediate

**Types**
General English

**Aims**
Distinguish between
similar idioms

**Class Time**
15-20 minutes

**Preparation Time**
45-60 minutes

**Resources**
List of difficult idioms

This activity is best planned with idioms relevant to particular places, age groups, and interests. There is room for the imagination to go to work on planning the grids.

## Procedure

1. Draw up a list of tricky idioms. Put the complementary parts of the idiom *make/do* (e.g., *make noise*) in bingo grids (see Appendix).
2. Distribute the grids to the class and review one idiom by choosing a complement from a grid you have kept for yourself. Write on it the board: *I _____ the dishes this morning.* When students respond *did*, ask them, *Did you do the dishes this morning?* If someone answers *yes*, cross out that complement on your grid and show the class. Students can proceed to formulate questions using *make/do* and find classmates who answer the target question affirmatively. Bingo rules apply. The first person to get five Xs in a row is the winner.
3. Sample target question frames include: *Did you . . . this morning?*, *Have you ever . . . ?*, *Can you . . . ?*, *Will you . . . after class?* Choose the target frame that is appropriate to the level and idiom and that produces natural language. This also calls for care in selecting the complements.

## Caveats and Options

1. Any grammar or idiom book can provide you with plenty of idiom pairs.
2. Make one empty Bingo grid and run off several copies before filling them. Label each blank grid *A, B, C,* and then fill them randomly, scrambling the idioms and/or changing the complements. Then run off an equal number of copies of each grid.

**Appendix:
Sample Bingo
Grid for
*Make/Do***

| | | | | |
|---|---|---|---|---|
| silly noises coffee | the bed a good job | the dishes a lot of money | your homework business in (e.g., Asia) | lunch

a shopping list |
| your laundry | a big mistake | free fun | anything | the exercise on page 24 |
| a suggestion | a mess | a phone call home | gardening | any friends at school |
| the vacuuming | anybody a favor | pancakes | a paper airplane | a scene |

**Contributor**

*Dennis Bricault is director of ESL Programs at North Park College, Chicago, in the United States. He has worked as a teacher/administrator in Spain, Hungary, and the United States.*

# Sharing Experiences

**Levels**
Intermediate +

**Types**
General English

**Aims**
Reflect on own attitudes
and aspects of social
settings
Use language associated
with feelings
Exchange information
and experiences
Make friends

**Class Time**
20–30 minutes during
four successive lessons

**Preparation Time**
10 minutes

**Resources**
Copies of blank grid

O n the first day of a new class, an activity like this one can break the ice without intruding into people's lives.

## Procedure

1. If the class is an advanced-level speaking class, hand out copies of the Sharing Experiences grid (see Appendix) and ask students to fill it in for homework. Have intermediate-level classes fill it in during class if they need help with vocabulary.
2. During the following class, put students into groups of two, three, or four to share information.
3. Discuss with students the most interesting fact they learned in their group.

## Caveats and Options

1. If advanced students have plenty to share, one horizontal line per class is the best way to present the material.
2. A class discussion after the sharing is optional.
3. Variants of this are easily constructed for ESP programs. The Appendix gives one example.

## Appendix: Sharing Experiences

*Instructions:* Fill in as much of this as you can and then share your answers with one, two, or three other people before we have a class or group discussion.

| Which things . . . | Impress you? | Confuse you? | Surprise you? | Amuse you? | Annoy you? | Worry you? |
|---|---|---|---|---|---|---|
| In New Zealand? | | | | | | |
| In your own/previous country | | | | | | |
| At work/ school/ university | | | | | | |

**Contributor**

*Dorothy Brown has been a teacher trainer at Auckland University, New Zealand, and in Sydney, Australia. She also teaches advanced English conversation and discussion classes.*

# Hmmmm!

**Levels**
Intermediate +

**Types**
Private language school

**Aims**
Hear and see the
importance of
intonation in
pronunciation
Determine the
difference in meaning
intonation makes with
various fillers
Use fillers properly in
conversation

**Class Time**
1 hour

**Preparation Time**
30 minutes

**Resources**
Blank copy of matrix
chart to be filled in by
students

ESL students need to understand the crucial role that intonation plays in making their pronunciation intelligible. One interesting and even fun way of driving this home is to look at the difference in meaning that occurs when we change the intonation on fillers (e.g., *hmm, oh-oh, ugh*).

## Procedure

1. Talk about the various levels of pronunciation, including the difference between segmentals (individual phonemes) and suprasegmentals (such as intonation). Discuss the importance of intonation in making pronunciation intelligible.
2. Hand out a sample matrix (see Appendix). Review the pronunciation of each filler with the various intonation patterns.
3. Assign students the task of finding out what those fillers mean. (Some intonation patterns will not work with some fillers). They can do this with a host family, an English-speaking friend, a work associate, or a stranger on the street, depending on how bold they are. Tell students that they will have to reproduce correctly the intonation patterns in order to get the correct answers.

## Caveats and Options

1. Have students write a short skit or play using a certain number of these fillers. Humorous situations can be devised by using the wrong intonation patterns. See how creative your students can be with this.

## Appendix: Sample Chart

| FILLER | LEVEL | RISE | FALL | RISE-FALL | FALL-RISE |
|---|---|---|---|---|---|
| ah | "Wait a minute" | | satisfaction | understanding | |
| eh | | "What was that?" or "Isn't that true? (tag question) | "What are you doing?" (anger) | | |
| gee | | | anger, disappointment | surprise | |
| hmm/ mmm | "I'm thinking" | "What did you say?" or "I don't think so." | agreement, understanding or "Let me see" | agreement, understanding or "Let me see" | |
| huh | | "What did you say?" or "I don't think so" | agreement, understanding or "Let me see" | | |
| oh | | surprise | disappointment (short) understanding (long) | excitement | puzzlement |
| oh-oh | | | | concern | warning |
| | | | | | |

| FILLER | LEVEL | RISE | FALL | RISE-FALL | FALL-RISE |
|---|---|---|---|---|---|
| okay | | agreement, under-standing (waiting for more) | agreement, under-standing (finished) | agreement, under-standing (finished) | agreement, under-standing (waiting for more) |
| ooo (/u/) | | | disgust | excite-ment | |
| so | | "Get to the point" | starting a new topic | | |
| ugh | | | anger, disgust, frustration | | |
| uh/um | pause | | | | |
| uh-uh | "No" (disinter-est) | "No" (interest—waiting for more) | "No" | "No" (defiance) | "No" (interest—waiting for more) |

## Contributor

*Mark Dickens is a freelance writer, editor, and ESL teacher who lives in Victoria, BC, Canada, where he most recently taught at Fields College International.*

# Establishing Rapport

**Levels**
Any

**Types**
Private language school

**Aims**
Improve the working relationship with the teacher

**Class Time**
None

**Preparation Time**
None

**Resources**
Social time outside the classroom

Adult learners appreciate social contact with their teacher. This may appear initially as a burden to the teacher but in fact should be considered as an investment because it will result in a better classroom atmosphere and thus facilitate learning. Investing a little of your social time with your adult learners turns students who may resent their role as a student in the class into cooperative friends of the teacher.

## Procedure

In the course introduction, use the following ice breaker:

1. Provide a handout with gaps for filling in personal information (see below).

| Name of student | Weekend activities | Means of transport | Preferred reading material | Hopes for this class | Other |
|---|---|---|---|---|---|
|  |  |  |  |  |  |
|  |  |  |  |  |  |
|  |  |  |  |  |  |
|  |  |  |  |  |  |

2. Have students interview each other and complete the form.

3. Have students use the form to introduce each other to the class.

4. Collect the forms and familiarize yourself with some of the information.

5. Make time to socialize with your students (e.g., before the lesson begins, during breaks, after class). Use the information provided in the personal information form to make small talk, for example: *How's your daughter these days? Have you found a new apartment yet? Did you go windsurfing at the weekend?*

6. Use this time to allow your students to gain insights into your own personal details.

7. Build on this sharing of information in your lesson when possible.

## Contributors

*David Gardner is senior language instructor in the English Centre of the University of Hong Kong. Lindsay Miller is assistant professor in the English Department at City University of Hong Kong.*

# The Cost of Living

**Levels**
Any

**Types**
Any

**Aims**
Develop conversational skills, specifically agreeing/disagreeing, interrupting, showing surprise, asking questions, and using fillers

**Class Time**
1-2 hours

**Preparation Time**
30 minutes

**Resources**
Handout
Shopping mall

Students in a foreign country are generally aware of the difference between the cost of living in their host country and that of their own. The teacher can capitalize on this real-life experience (and concern) by using it as a discussion topic. Students are also motivated to talk about things that are relevant to their own lives and with which they have some experience.

## Procedure

1. At the end of a lesson, ask a few students if they know the cost of a pound or kilo of tomatoes, a quart of milk, a Big Mac, a compact disk and so on in Chicago or Sydney (or wherever they are living).
2. Distribute handout (see Appendix) and ask the students to go on a window shopping trip to their nearest shopping mall and fill in the prices on the items on the handout. Ask students to fill in the second column on the handout giving a rough idea of the cost of these items in their own countries.
3. In the next lesson, tell the students that they are going to have a discussion. You may want to preteach some conversational skills that are useful in discussions (e.g., agreeing/disagreeing, interrupting, showing surprise, asking questions, using fillers). Arrange students into groups of three or four, making sure that each group includes different nationalities.
4. Have a discussion based on the information on their handout. Circulate and encourage students to go beyond a simple description of the information (e.g., *Why are tomatoes so cheap in Mexico? Do many people buy fast food in Thailand? Are compact discs popular everywhere in Egypt?*).

5. When it seems that the groups are ready to end their discussions, ask some of the students to give their general impressions of the cost of living in other countries. Ask if anything surprised them. The discussion could them be widened to include the possible reasons for the differences in the cost of living in certain countries.

## Caveats and Options

1. This activity could be the basis for a writing task. After completing the handout, students could write letters to friends in their home countries telling them about how expensive or cheap it is to live in the United States.

## Appendix: Sample Handout

*Directions:* Use this table to compare the prices of things in the shops where you live now with the prices that you remember from your own country.

| | Cost in U.S. ($) | Approximate cost in my country (U.S.$) |
|---|---|---|
| 1 pound or kilo of tomatoes | | |
| a quart of milk | | |
| a lettuce | | |
| a Big Mac | | |
| a compact disc | | |
| a T-shirt | | |

## Contributors

*Lindsay Miller is assistant professor in the English Department at City University of Hong Kong. David Gardner is senior instructor in the English Centre at the University of Hong Kong.*

# Preparing the Family Budget

**Levels**
Beginner–intermediate

**Types**
General English
conversation classes
On-arrival English
classes for new
immigrants

**Aims**
Become accustomed to
cost of goods in the
new country
Use reference material
and telephone calls to
find information
Improve conversational
fluency

**Class Time**
3 hours

**Preparation Time**
1 hour

**Resources**
Budget form
Local newspapers
Phone directories
Calculator for each
group (optional)

This is an activity for students who need to find out about the basics of living on a budget in a new country.

## Procedure

1. Divide students into groups of no more than four people.
2. Explain that they will be preparing a budget for their imaginary family and that they must come to an agreement on how to spend their money. Instruct the students to be as realistic as possible. Provide each group with a budget form and a task prompt (see Appendix).
3. Discuss unfamiliar vocabulary.
4. Give students a few minutes to talk in their groups about what they need to find out to be able to accomplish the task.
5. Conduct a whole-class brainstorming session on information needed and resources available. (See Appendix for a list of possibilities.)
6. Have students work in class using resources available, then divide up any telephone calls or additional information gathering for outside the class.
7. Allow some time the second day for students to compile their research and reach a consensus on how to budget the family income.
8. Have each group present their decisions and reasons for allocations of money.

## Caveats and Options

1. If the students are not comfortable using the telephone, consider arranging for some "plants" who are willing to be available to take calls regarding such things as car insurance costs.

2. Help students identify what they will need to know before making calls (e.g., to insure a car they will be asked the make, model, and year of the car, and what their driving record is).
3. Have extra budget forms available if students want to use them for their personal budgets. They should not be required to hand these in, however, because this is private information.
4. To get an estimate of food costs, the groups might come up with a weekly shopping list and price the items at the local market.
5. A field trip could be arranged to the grocery store to obtain prices.
6. You should be available to provide language but should not interfere. This is a good opportunity to listen for problems that could be the source of future lessons.
7. To make the activity suitable for less advanced students, supply some or all of the cost data.

## Appendix: Family Budget Situation

*Task:* You live in a family of three people: husband, wife, and 5-year-old child. The husband earns $30,000 per year or $2,500 per month. The wife does not work. The standard deductions taken from the husband's pay check each month have been figured for you. You will be living in the Unites States for 18 months. Before you leave, you would like to take a tour of the country. You think it will cost about $3,500. Based on the net income, prepare a budget for your family. Can you take the vacation you want? Can you expand it? Will you have to reduce it?

Family Budget

|  | One month |
| --- | --- |
| Gross income | 2,500.00 |
| Federal tax | 449.17 |
| State tax | 128.33 |
| FICA | 191.25 |
| Insurance | 108.33 |
| Credit Union |  |
| Uniforms |  |
| Union dues |  |
| Retirement |  |

| | |
|---|---|
| Total deductions | 877.08 |
| Net income | 1,622.92 |
| Rent | _____ |
| Car payment | _____ |
| Utilities | _____ |
| Telephone | _____ |
| Gasoline | _____ |
| Food | _____ |
| Entertainment | _____ |
| Clothing | _____ |
| Gifts | _____ |
| Household items | _____ |
| Cleaning/laundry | _____ |
| Savings | _____ |
| Car insurance | _____ |
| Other | _____ |
| Total expenses | _____ |

Suggested Resources for Preparing the Family Budget

Classified section of local newspaper
Family
Apartment managers
Trip to the grocery store
Insurance salesperson
Telephone company representative
Trip to a cleaners and a laundromat
Drive by a gasoline station (gallons may be unfamiliar)
Trip to the mall
Utility company representative

**Contributor**

*Vicki Melin Schoen is currently a graduate student at Georgia State University, in Atlanta, Georgia, in the United States. She is pursuing an MA in applied linguistics and ESL.*

# Communicating With the Boss

**Levels**
Advanced

**Types**
English for professional
purposes

**Aims**
Practice writing concise,
effective memos
Review and analyze own
work
Help each other
improve work
Learn an appropriate
communication
technique for having
dialogue with a
supervisor

**Class Time**
1–2 hours

**Preparation Time**
5–20 minutes

**Resources**
Several written
situations
Instructions for Step 7

Writing memos in a workplace calls for skills as well as understanding of the supervisor-worker relationship. Examples can be collected from real-life situations.

## Procedure

1. Have students review several workplace conflict situations (see Appendix A) and brainstorm appropriate ways of handling the issue and getting the results they want from a supervisor.
2. Show students an example of a business memo and be sure they understand the purpose and form. Be sure they understand, too, the difference between making a specific request through a memo (e.g., *May we talk about this?*) and an effort to solve the entire issue through the memo.
3. Divide students into groups of three or four.
4. Have each group member describe a situation.
5. Ask students to write a memo to their supervisor defining the problem and requesting specific action. The memo should be no longer than one page. This can be done as homework. Encourage students to evaluate and revise their own work to be sure the meaning is clear.
6. Make enough copies of each memo so that every group member has a copy of all memos written by their group members. Next, have students act as the supervisor and respond to each request.
7. Give a copy of the response instructions to each person (see Appendix B). Review the instructions orally, answering any questions concerning them. Tell the students to use these instructions as a basis for responding to each memo in writing. This can be assigned as homework.

8. Put students in their assigned groups and have them discuss each memo using their written responses to work from. They should ask clarifying questions so they can understand how to get a positive response from a superior. They should take special note of the paraphrases to be sure the reader got the intended meaning.
9. Have students rewrite their memos incorporating any suggestions they think are valuable.
10. After the rewrite, review the memos using the criteria that have been established for written work.

## Caveats and Options

1. The responses could come back in the form of memos.
2. The writing form and subjects could change and become, for example, a letter addressed to you.
3. This could be converted to an oral activity with the students roleplaying the employee and the boss.
4. Students could make up their own situations based on real experience.
5. The peer response is intended to provide useful feedback. If students have difficulty expressing honest feedback orally, skip the discussion part and rely only on the written response; if students are comfortable with oral feedback, you might want to eliminate the written portion.

## Appendix A: Situations for Communicating With the Boss

1. You have heard that a key customer is having serious financial trouble. You are aware that your company is dependent on this customer to maintain a strong cash flow.
2. You have just received additional assignments with short deadlines. You already have a full work load with responsibility for the completion of two key projects. The projects are on schedule, but several components require a lot of time during the following 2 weeks.
3. You have heard that a competitor is going out of business. If this is true, it should provide your company with new opportunities.
4. You think that your company is missing part of its market.

## Appendix B: Instructions for Communicating With the Boss

## Contributor

5. You have noticed an area of plant safety which you do not believe will meet government safety and health standards. It will cost money and manpower to correct. You do not have the authority to allocate either to the job.

1. Paraphrase the request.
2. Does the memo give you enough information to respond? If not, what more do you need?
3. Is there more information than you need to know to make a decision on the request?
4. How would you handle the request?
5. Why?

*Vicki Melin Schoen is currently a graduate student at Georgia State University in Atlanta, Georgia, in the United States. She is pursuing an MA in applied linguistics and ESL.*

# Learning to Learn

**Levels**
Intermediate

**Types**
Private language school
short term courses in
general English

**Aims**
Get to know new
students
Exchange learning
strategies

**Class Time**
40 minutes

**Preparation Time**
10 minutes

**Resources**
Worksheet

Exchanging learning strategies in class is a good way of making students realize that many ideas come from within their own group.

## Procedure

1. Hand out the worksheets (see Appendix).
2. Explain that students are to collect other people's ideas and names.
3. Ask students to report back one idea each that they would like to try for themselves.
4. Use the answers throughout the week as part of your lessons.

## Appendix: Autograph Hunt

*Directions:* Find a different person to finish each sentence. Ask your classmates to write their names after their sentences.

The best way to learn new words is to _____

*Name* _____

If you feel nervous about talking in English you should _____

*Name* _____

When I'm reading and I don't understand a word I _____

*Name* _____

A good way to give yourself listening practice is to _____

*Name* _____

My favorite way of reviewing grammar points is to _____

*Name* _____

I practice writing in English by _____

*Name* _____

I use the English language tapes from the textbook like this:_____

*Name* _____

One good idea for reviewing lessons is to _____

*Name* _____

## Caveats and Options

1. Have students make suggestions for sentence starters for the following week's activity.

## Contributor

*Gregory Turner teaches at a private language school in Auckland, New Zealand, and is currently studying for a Diploma in English Language Teaching. Previously, he taught in Japan.*

Part VI: Word Prompts

*Yousif Murad at Northern Virginia Community College, Alexandria, Virginia USA.*

# Introduction

An interesting range of language learning activities can be generated simply with word prompts, spoken or written. In this section, teachers show how words can start a lesson on topics as varied as basic literacy or literature, chatting, or formal speechmaking.

# What If . . .

**Levels**
Intermediate +

**Types**
Continuous education
or an advanced-level
conversation course

**Aims**
Discuss appropriate
options in difficult
situations

**Class Time**
30 minutes

**Preparation Time**
30–45 minutes

**Resources**
Handout

Students must take into account cultural attitudes and typical responses in their interactions with native English speakers in order to avoid miscommunication. In this activity, students have the opportunity to discuss cultural misunderstandings.

## Procedure

1. Introduce students to the topic of cultural misunderstandings. Reveal a personal experience or ask one or two students for their own experience(s).
2. Depending on class size, organize students into groups of three.
3. Distribute the handout (or one of your own) to each student, and direct the students to decide on a course of action in response to each question (see Appendix).
4. Finally, have each group discuss their decision with the class as a whole. You may want to discuss what is considered appropriate in the host country.

## Caveats and Options

1. Write the questions out on slips of paper and put them into a hat or bag.
2. Each student then chooses a question and reads it aloud to the rest of the class.
3. The student must decide on a course of action.

## Appendix: Sample Handout

*Directions:* Discuss among yourselves an appropriate answer to each dilemma.

1. What would you do if you were invited to a friend's house and served a food that is taboo in your culture?
2. What would you do if you had to work on one of your most sacred holidays?
3. What would you do if you were in a fancy restaurant and bit into something that tasted horrible?
4. What would you do if your family disapproved of your best friend?
5. What would you say if you went to the movies and your friend found the film entertaining while you found it offensive?
6. What would you do if your teacher unintentionally asked you an embarrassing question in front of the other students?
7. What would you do if you saw a fellow student cheating (or a co-worker stealing from your company)?

## Contributor

*Lynne Alberts is working toward her MA in TESL at Georgia State University, in the United States. She has taught ESL as a volunteer through the Intensive English Program in Austin, Texas, and has tutored Spanish and French.*

# Hang on a Minute

**Levels**
High intermediate +

**Types**
Intensive English Language
Testing Service (IELTS) or
other English proficiency
examination preparation
classes
English for academic
purposes, special purposes,
or general

**Aims**
Develop confidence in
speaking fluently and at
length in front of peers
Focus on a single topic
Listen critically to a
lengthy discourse, focusing
on fluency and relevance

**Class Time**
40–70 minutes

**Preparation Time**
Minimal

**Resources**
Stop watch
Small handbell
Pen and paper or
whiteboard marker
List of general topics of
interest to the particular
group of students

This activity is a simplified version of the BBC radio program *Just a Minute*. I have found it particularly valuable for students preparing for the International English Language Testing Service (IELTS) Oral Interview on a number of levels:

- as a challenge to speak fluently and meaningfully for 1 minute on a topic of general, everyday interest
- as an opportunity to practice and experiment with key structural and grammatical features of spoken English in a relaxed way
- as a welcome break from the relentless and stressful grind of more pedestrian oral exercises.

## Procedure

1. Divide class into Team A and Team B. Act as adjudicator, referee, and score-keeper.
2. Arrange tables and chairs so that the teams face each other. Sit at the head of the two tables, like this:

   Teacher

   | | |
   |-----|-----|
   | A1 | B1 |
   | A2 | B2 |
   | A3 | B3 |
   | A4 | B4 |

3. Explain the object of the game. Assign roles and tasks:

   Designated Speaker (DS)
   - speaks to the rest of the team members of both sides for 1 minute
   - avoids losing the topic to an opponent by not hesitating or wandering off the topic

146

- scores points for being the person who is still speaking at the end of 1 minute.

Members of Opposing Team
- listen carefully to the DS's talk
- interrupt the DS if he or she hesitates or wanders off the topic
- states clearly to the two teams the reason for the interruption (hesitation or lack of relevance in DS's talk).

4. Nominate Student A1 as the DS to speak on the first topic thus:

   Student A1 will speak to us for 1 minute on the subject of horses without hesitating or wandering off the subject. (Pause for 10 seconds so DS can collect his or her thoughts). Beginning . . . now.

5. Start the stop watch.

6. Allow Student A1 to continue speaking until any member of Team B notices a hesitation or irrelevance in Student A1's delivery.

7. Pause the stop watch as soon as a Team B member interrupts. Ask the interrupting Team B member why he or she challenged Student A1. Ask the challenging team member to offer a specific reason for the challenge, for example:

   Not relevant: She's not talking about horses; she's talking about her favorite dog.
   Hesitation: He said, "Errrr . . . "

8. Adjudicate the challenge.

   If you agree with the challenge, award a point to Team B. Say, for example: "I agree with the challenge. Student B1, you have 45 seconds left on the subject of horses." The successful challenging student from Team B takes up the same subject for the remainder of the time on the stop watch. Or the new speaker can begin to speak on the subject in any way she or he likes, as long as she or he is relevant and does not hesitate.

   If you disagree with the challenge: Award a point to Team A. Student A1 can then continue with the same subject for the remainder of the time on the stop watch. Or Student A1 can continue the talk or begin to speak on the subject in a different way if desired, as long as he or she is relevant and does not hesitate.

9. Allow Team B to continue to challenge at any time. The same rules for challenges apply each time a challenge is made.
10. Ring a bell at the end of the minute on the stop watch. Award two points to the student speaking at the end of the minute.

## Caveats and Options

1. Emphasize to participants that the game is not a race. Speed is not fluency.
2. Students will find that it takes a little time to adjust to the strict requirements of relevance and fluency. Do not apply the rules relating to hesitation too rigorously during the first couple of sessions.
3. Do not interrupt, except when demonstrating for the first time.
4. For a warm-up exercise students can practice speaking in pairs. Provide a topic for a 30 seconds nonstop talk for each partner. Increase this to 1 minute.
5. Larger classes (16+) can be divided into two groups for simultaneous games.
6. Teams can choose appropriate or popular names for their team.
7. As students become more adept at the game, competitions can be held between teams of two or three. This increases the responsibility of each student to pick up contraventions of the rules and gives more opportunity to each student to speak.
8. Where multiple games are in progress, each game will require a referee equipped with a stop watch to arbitrate. Needless to say, the referee has the last word in cases of disputes.
9. Students may compile the list of general topics of interest as a preliminary warm-up activity to the main game.

## Contributor

*Russell Allthorpe is a TESOL academic at the Defence International Training Centre, Melbourne, Australia; an International English Language Testing Services examiner; and is currently completing his MA (TESOL) at Deakin University.*

# Writing Affectively (sic)

**Levels**
Advanced

**Types**
Academic preparation
course

**Aims**
Exploit the affective
element in writing
Develop a framework
and skills for ongoing
formal writing
Break through
mechanistic approaches
to academic writing

**Class Time**
45 minutes

**Preparation Time**
None

**Resources**
Envelope with small
cards, each with a one-
or two-word topic on it

This task approaches academic writing creatively by building into it randomness and spontaneity. It also encourages students to think beyond a strict paragraph/essay organization, which tends to limit many in developing their academic writing.

## Procedure

1. Model the activity thoroughly the first time you do it. Make clear that:
   - students have a total of 20 minutes for the exercise
   - they are not to worry about paragraphing—this can come later if they choose to work further on this piece
   - the purpose is to get them writing and to break down blocks they may have—accuracy is irrelevant at this stage.
2. Have one student pick a topic at random from the envelope.
3. Have students take out a blank sheet of paper, preferably turning it sideways, (to discourage linear thinking), write the topic in the center of the page, and circle it.
4. Ask students to develop clusters of words radiating from this central topic following random thought. Some words will develop into branches as related words occur; others may not. This phase takes a few minutes at most.
5. As soon as students feel ready, tell them to begin to write. Not all of the generated words will be used—in fact, some may write about a small section of their diagram only. Write at the same time that students are writing.
6. At 20 minutes, tell students to stop writing.
7. Go around the class, having everyone, including you, read his or her work in turn. Anyone who does not wish to read may pass.
8. The first few times, ask for feedback and discuss what students found helpful or otherwise about the activity.

## Caveats and Options

1. This is personal writing and needs to be treated sensitively.
2. I have found it useful to go through the process along with students. This seems to increase the sense of writing as exploration and thus encourages students to reflect on aspects of the writing process.
3. Strictly limiting the time is frustrating for some students but encourages students to get to work quickly. The time limit seems to make the task less daunting by removing the responsibility for producing a completed piece of work—which helps reduce writer's block.
4. This method leads into essay planning. Once students are used to the clustering technique, they can use it for brainstorming and organizing ideas for essay writing. It helps ideas flow and also helps students visualize connections between ideas.
5. Students are encouraged to use this method outside of class for additional writing practice. Topics may be chosen at random from nearby objects, sights, and so on or from lists of essay topics for timed practice writing.
6. Where this method is used in conjunction with other writing techniques, such as formal essay writing and speed copying, students are encouraged to keep a reflective journal to record their responses to writing tasks and evaluation of their own writing process.
7. As a follow-up, those who wish may hand in their work for feedback on specific areas. Some will choose to work over what they have written at home. At this stage they may choose to develop the writing into a more formal essay.

## References and Further Reading

Rico, G. L. (1983). *Writing the natural way.* New York: Tarcher/Perigee.

## Contributor

*Marion Bagot teaches ESOL at Hornsby College of Technical and Further Education (TAFE) vocational programs, in Sydney, Australia.*

# Looks Familiar

**Levels**
Beginning +

**Types**
General English

**Aims**
Recognize cognates and
false friends

**Class Time**
5–15 minutes

**Preparation Time**
30– 65 minutes

**Resources**
Newspaper ads,
magazines, pamphlets,
and brochures
Photocopier
List of cognates
common to English and
the students' L1(s)
List of false cognates

Beginning-level students are often both motivated and intimidated by a new language. By showing students that English contains numerous cognates, you can help them build their vocabulary and confidence. More advanced learners can benefit from this activity by becoming aware of false cognates or "false friends."

## Procedure

1. Research some potential cognates that the students' L1(s) may share with English (e.g., months, foods, brand names). A foreign-language dictionary or a fluent speaker of that language are good places to start.
2. After compiling a list of words (e.g., months, foods, brand names), look for examples in newspaper ads, brochures, and magazines. Make photocopies or overhead projector (OHP) transparencies.
3. Divide the students into small groups (two or three students) and give each group one photocopy. Ask them to circle every word they know (true beginners) or every word their language shares with English (low beginning–advanced).
4. Use the board or OHP transparencies to present or follow up the activity: Write words on board (or circle words on OHP) and discuss. Extend the activity by adding words.

## Caveats and Options

1. This activity works best in monolingual classes in which the teacher has a working knowledge of the students' language. Because such a situation is not always the case, you can use international words for

products (e.g., *walkman*), brand names (e.g., *General Electric*), and places (e.g., *McDonald's*) to teach pronunciation and new vocabulary.

2. This activity could be done as an experiment. Ask students to develop lists of cognates (and false friends or tricky words). Keep the lists (arranged by language) for future reference.

## References and Further Reading

Hill, R. J. (1982). *Dictionary of false friends.* London: Macmillan.

## Contributor

*Dennis Bricault is the director of ESL Programs and an instructor in Spanish at North Park College, in Illinois, in the United States. He is currently pursuing a doctorate in higher education administration.*

# Words to Poems to Drama

**Levels**
Intermediate +

**Types**
Semester-long classes
with a stable enrollment

**Aims**
Use language creatively

**Class Time**
50–60 minutes

**Preparation Time**
30 minutes

**Resources**
Individual words written
on separate slips of
paper (enough for each
pair of students to have
up to 16 words)

Creativity can be low in language classes if students are concentrating on writing correctly. Poetry writing, on the other hand, allows them to be free of some of the constraints of making complete sentences.

## Procedure

1.  Pair off students (or form groups of three if necessary). Give each pair paper and pen.
2.  Randomly select 10 words from the collection and write them on the board. Explain that they will be using these words to write poems, and that there is no limit to the number of words to a line.
3.  Ask each pair to work together to group words that seem to complement each other, then to group words that sound good together. Here, stress that making sense is not the primary objective.
4.  Assign new partners. Give each pair a random selection of words (approximately 16). Have each pair rearrange the words until they find a form they like and then copy their poem onto a piece of paper.
5.  Have each pair sit with another pair, and then have each person in the group of four read aloud each poem. Ask students to discuss the word groupings and whether they have heard these words together before. Ask each group to think of the images they are creating.
6.  Again, assign new partners. Give each pair approximately 12 words. Again, ask them to use the words to create a poem and copy it. This time they work out a way for it to be read aloud by both of them to the class. Will they read all of it together? Will one of them read part of it and the other one read the rest? Will they make it into a conversation? Have them decide and present it to the class.

7. One last time, assign new partners. Give each pair 12 words and again ask them to create a poem. This time tell students to incorporate movement into the presentation. Instead of vocalizing all the words, they may use movement. They may repeat words or use one voice or two at any given time, but both students must be actively involved in the presentation.

**Caveats and Options**

1. Each time the students change partners, it is a new session, and each session may be repeated several times until students are confident enough to move on.

**Contributor**

*Aileen Davidson is working on her MA thesis in applied linguistics at Victoria University of Wellington, New Zealand. She tutors on the writing course at the English Language Institute and has been a drama tutor for 20 years.*

# Neighborhood Signs

**Levels**
Beginning–intermediate

**Types**
Private language school

**Aims**
Decipher and interpret
typical signs around the
neighborhood
Figure out abbreviations
or special phrases used
in posted signs

**Class Time**
1 hour

**Preparation Time**
1 hour

**Resources**
Handout with
transcribed text from
some signs (no pictures)

S tudents commonly see signs that they may not understand because of specific abbreviations or phrases that only native speakers are familiar with. Signs are a specific genre of text that, apart from those involving graphic images, are not often covered in ESL classrooms. This activity gives students needed practice with the language of signs.

## Procedure

1. Go around your neighborhood and note the text of some signs that you see (e.g., *Vehicles and contents left at owner's risk, Max headroom 6 ft.*). Type these minitexts on a handout.
2. Put the students in groups of two or three and ask them to try and identify where they would see each of the signs and what they mean, including any abbreviations or special phrases.
3. Discuss the sign texts as a class, pointing out any cultural background necessary for understanding.

## Caveats and Options

1. The students can go out and collect the texts from the neighborhood (or bring some from the neighborhoods where they live).

## Contributor

*Mark Dickens is a freelance writer, editor, and ESL teacher who lives in Victoria, British Columbia, Canada, where he most recently taught at Fields College International.*

# Sequenced Microthemes for Advanced ESL Writers

**Levels**
Advanced

**Types**
Undergraduate and
graduate writing
programs

**Aims**
Write and revise essays
Organize ideas before
writing
Analyze and synthesize
information for
academic writing

**Class Time**
Eight 2-hour classes

**Preparation Time**
Time spent reading
essays and providing
comments

**Resources**
Selected microthemes

This approach to writing represents a sequence of microthemes—issues in family life that deal with the central theme of culture. It makes use of reading prompts to provide topics for writing and draws upon the adult students' existing knowledge of their own culture. This course was developed especially for students whose English proficiency test results indicate a need for skill improvement in writing only.

## Procedure

1. Provide microtheme on a handout (see Appendix).
2. Discuss the theme, suggesting different approaches that the students may take in their writing.
3. Have students write the essay during class.
4. Use class time also as an opportunity to meet with students individually to discuss your comments on previous essays. Have students revise their essays outside of class.

## Caveats and Options

1. The microthemes given in the Appendix were developed for a program in the United States; however, they can be adapted for use in other English-speaking cultures.
2. Sequenced microthemes can also be used in an integrated-skills classroom where several readings on one theme provide a prompt for discussion and writing. They can also be used in a course that has a predetermined content.
3. Two or more microthemes may be incorporated into one longer paper at the end of the course.

4. Microthemes may be assigned in a specific sequence to present those less cognitively demanding at first.
5. Writing could be done in a computer lab if facilities are available; however, inadequate keyboard skills may hamper the writing process.

Leeds, B. (Ed.). (1996). *Writing in a second language: Insights from first and second language teaching and research.* London: Longman.

**References and Further Reading**

# Appendix: Selected Microthemes

1. Impressions of the United States in Your Country

People around the world have different impressions of the United States and the American people. Some of these impressions are favorable while others are not. Often they are formed as a result of the culture the United States exports through books, films, TV programs, news reports, merchandise, and tourists. How does the United States export its culture to your country? Based on your experience, do you agree with the impression of the United States and Americans in your country?

2. Role of Women in Society

Discuss the role of women in society from either of the following perspectives.
- a comparison between your country and the United States
- a comparison between your parents' or grandparents' generation and your generation in your country.

*[Note: The choice of perspectives accommodates varying amounts of experience with the host culture.]*

3. Family Relationships

In an increasingly mobile society, it is difficult for the different generations in some families to maintain a close relationship. Yet when older family members become ill or are unable to care for themselves, they may need help from their children. As more women today work outside the home and family members have hectic daily schedules, caring for an elderly person can place a strain on family relationships. In your culture, are sons and daughters expected to be responsible for the care of their aging parents?

4. Social Problems

Did you know that poverty and homelessness are major social issues in the United States today? Discuss one or two social problems in your country. What efforts have been made, if any, to address them?
*[Note: The teacher may expand upon current problems in the host society and efforts being made to resolve them.]*

5. Melting Pot versus Salad Bowl (Ethnicity as enrichment or divisiveness)

In Country X, there exist several races and ethnic groups. Over the years, there has been tension among these groups and some episodes of violence. Some of the groups are trying to maintain their individual cultures including languages and traditions. Many of these people were immigrants to country X or are descendants of immigrants. The largest groups have demanded that their identities be officially recognized, for example, by having documents issued in more than one language and by allowing their children to be educated in their first language.

One might argue that immigration to a new country involves assimilation to the host culture, creating one national identity, like a melting pot. A multiethnic society where different cultures and languages are promoted may be considered a divisive one. On the other hand, one might use the term *salad bowl* to describe a region in which different groups coexist, but continue to preserve individual identities, believing that this situation enriches life for everyone.

Based on the above, respond to one of the following:

- Could this Country X be your country (either now or at some point in its history), or another country you know? If so, describe the situation. In your opinion, is a multiethnic society always a divisive one? or

- If you are unfamiliar with such a situation, address the following question: How does or would your country view cultural/linguistic diversity, as enrichment or divisiveness?

*[Note: Additional time may be allotted for this topic.]*

## Acknowledgment

I thank Ray Smith of the Campus-Wide Writing Program at Indiana University for suggesting the term *sequenced microthemes*.

**Contributor**

*Debra Hardison is a doctoral candidate in linguistics and an ESL instructor at Indiana University, in Pennsylvania, in the United States. She has published in* Language Learning, The Canadian Modern Language Review, *and various collections.*

# Okay, You Can Go

**Levels**
Beginning–intermediate

**Types**
Any

**Aims**
Produce a target
structure

**Class Time**
1–2 minutes

**Preparation Time**
None

**Resources**
None

Here is an easy way to review particular structures and liven up the end of a lesson.

## Procedure

1. Ask a student a question designed to produce a target structure, preferably one taught in a recent lesson. For example, to produce the short answer *Yes, I do* or *No, I don't*, you might ask, *Do you like chocolate?*
2. Allow students to go if the target structure is produced. Tell the students to stay if they fail to produce the target structure.
3. Proceed quickly around the class, asking every student a different question.
4. Return to those who answered incorrectly the first time.

## Caveats and Options

1. The questions need to be asked quickly, as students are generally eager to leave by the end of a lesson.

## Contributor

*John Macalister is establishing an English language program for the Auckland Institute of Technology at the Institute of Technology of Cambodia, Phnom Penh.*

# Dialogues in Action

**Levels**
High beginning–low intermediate

**Types**
Intensive ESL in a community college or university setting

**Aims**
Improve listening and speaking skills in a meaningful context

**Class Time**
30–45 minutes

**Preparation Time**
30–60 minutes

**Resources**
Computer and printer
Graphics program for illustrations (optional)

The audiolingual method relied heavily on dialogue memorization to improve students' speaking and listening skills. Today, we acknowledge that listening is a creative activity requiring learners to process linguistic input and apply it to existing schema. This activity illustrates how to adapt and create spoken interchanges to allow creativity on the part of the students.

## Procedure

1. Pass out the dialogue on handouts (see Appendix).
2. Read it through and have students repeat.
3. Ask students to roleplay in groups and individually. Have students make changes as they take turns using their names and their own situations.
4. Next, have students make up their own dialogues or parts of dialogues as a follow-up activity.

## Caveats and Options

1. Teachers should be alert to problems that face learners such as cross-association of similar items. In some languages, the idiom is *I have hunger* rather than *I am hungry*. Another problem is recalling information. Like the other language skills, speaking and listening need to be taught in order to acquaint the students with chunks of discourse in the English language. It is important to teach them the skills necessary to process the information without having them translate back into their own language.

2. Students can do a pronunciation activity as part of the exercise. Other variations include using a picture dictionary as a prompt for a dialogue.

## References and Further Reading

Anderson-Mejias, P. L. (1996). English for academic listening: Teaching the skills associated with listening to extended discourse. *Foreign Language Annals, 19*, 391–397.

Bowen, J. D., Madsen, H., & Hilferty, A. (1995). *TESOL techniques and procedures*. Rowley, MA: Newbury House.

## Appendix: Sample Handout

Conversation 1: The campus

| | |
|---|---|
| Fred: | "Hi Kim. How are you?" |
| Kim: | "I'm OK. How are you?" |
| Fred: | "I'm tired. Exams are next week." |
| Kim: | "I know. Are your classes hard?" |
| Fred: | "Sometimes, but they are interesting." |
| Kim: | "Are you studying English?" |
| Fred: | "No. I am taking biology." |

Dialogue Completion:

1. Fred: "Hi Kim. _____ are you?"
2. Kim: "_____ OK. How are you?"
3. Fred: "I'm tired. Exams _____ next week."
4. Kim: "I know. Are your _____ hard?"
5. Fred: "Sometimes, but _____ are interesting."
6. Kim: "Are you _____ English?"
7. Fred: "No. I _____ taking biology."

*[Note: Now redo this somewhat with a change of players and scene. Students take parts and speak about what they are doing. They use their own names and talk about classes or other activities.]*

## Contributor

*Douglas Magrath teaches ESL at Seminole Community College and Embry-Riddle Aeronautical University. He also trains teachers for Lake County, Florida, in the United States.*

# Kill the Monday Morning Blues

*Levels*
Beginning–intermediate

*Types*
Any

*Aims*
Practice speaking and
listening skills in an
enjoyable group
atmosphere

*Class Time*
20 minutes

*Preparation Time*
5 minutes

*Resources*
Chairs

This activity works well as an ice breaker or rust remover after the weekend, particularly if students have not spoken much English since the previous class. It brings the group together, and they have fun. It can also be useful for review of particular structures or tenses. It promotes keen listening skills and can be used to focus on accuracy.

## Procedure

1. Have students arrange their chairs in a circle with you standing in the center.
2. Ask them to remember what they did at the weekend.
3. Tell students that you are going to ask some of them to change seats. Say, "If you went to the supermarket at the weekend, change seats." Check comprehension if necessary by asking a few individuals, "Did you go to the supermarket on Saturday or Sunday?" and showing them to another seat.
4. Sit down in one of the seats yourself while they are changing places, leaving one person without a seat, standing in the middle.
5. Ask this person to give instructions, for example, "If you drove a car, change seats." Help out at first to ensure students are using past tense and are understood by others.
6. Continue the game for 10–15 minutes with a new person left in the middle each time. There will be lots of laughter as well as opportunities for introducing or reinforcing new language and being creative.

**Caveats and Options**

1. Practice particular structures such as the present simple: *If you enjoy . . . , If you walk to . . .* and everyday routines: *If you get up before 8 o'clock . . . . , If you eat toast for breakfast . . . .*

2. If you wish to focus on accuracy, insist that nobody change seats until the instruction is grammatically correct. The student may self-correct or may need assistance from others.

**Contributor**

*Karen Margetts teaches ESOL in the Languages Unit at Otago Polytechnic, Dunedin, New Zealand. She has taught English and ESOL in high schools in New Zealand.*

# Pick a Topic

**Levels**
Any

**Types**
Any

**Aims**
Express interests in
classroom topics

**Class Time**
30–60 minutes

**Preparation Time**
15 minutes +

**Resources**
Lists of topics and
situations for students to
select from

In this activity, students indicate their preferences for topics to use in a new class. By doing this, they have some say in the content matter of the class, which is a common practice in adult education. When the subject matter of the class is of interest to the students, their interest in language learning grows and they feel more at ease.

## Procedure

1. Make a list of topics and situations that you have knowledge about, resources for, and perhaps that you think the students might be interested in. Compile a fairly comprehensive list so that the students have a wide choice of topics and situations.
2. Adapt the way you present the list to the students according to their language level. With beginning-level students, you may want to use their L1. However, you could be creative and use symbols for the topics too. For more advanced groups, have discussions or debates to decide the course content.
3. In class let the students choose the topics that are of special interest to them and then hand them in. You could even have another student or team of students compile the results and then present them to the class.
4. According to which topics have been indicated and the number of students, agree with the students as to which ones you will emphasize in the class. Try to make sure that everyone is reasonably satisfied.
5. Design a program around what the students have chosen. Popular topics often relate to travel (e.g., transportation, hotels, shopping, restaurants). Find and create activities to fit those topics and situations. Grammar comparisons can be done with transportation. Vocabulary exercises on a topic are good choices as well. You can also

read poems on the subject and roleplay. Teach language functions as well to fit the topics chosen.

## Caveats and Options

1. This activity takes time in that you have to plan a new program with each group. For this reason, it is important to consider how much you can realistically do. If you have enough resources on at least a few basic themes, you can use those themes for the initial list for the students to choose from.
2. Even for more structured academic classes this activity might have some merit, as with conversation courses, for example.
3. The students in some settings expect the teacher to take responsibility for the language development, so this activity provides a kind of happy medium: the teacher is the authority but the students help decide the themes to use in language instruction. By letting the students choose their topics and situations of interest, you also get a better idea of their goals in language learning.

## Contributor

*Margo Menconi is an English instructor in Bratsk, Russia. She is finishing her MA in adult education.*

# Enjoyable Ways of Reviewing Vocabulary

**Levels**
Any

**Types**
Short- or long-term
general English
ESP

**Aims**
Review recently learned
vocabulary

**Class Time**
5–60 minutes

**Preparation Time**
3 minutes for Games 1
and 2
10 minutes for Games 3
and 4

**Resources**
List of new vocabulary
words
Words on individual
cards (same number of
cards as there are
students) for Game 1
Two handouts per pair
for Game 3
Pairs of cards with word
and definition or
sentence containing the
word for Game 4

Students need continuous review of new vocabulary in order to use it productively. Review should be motivating, enjoyable, and varied so as to focus on different aspects of new vocabulary (e.g., meaning, use, collocations, pronunciation). It is even more fun if it is a competitive or cooperative experience.

## Procedure

Game 1: Horseshoes

1. Write review words (one per student) on individual cards.
2. Have students form two concentric circles, pairing up with a student in the other circle.
3. Give each pair two word cards and a table or chair to place them on.
4. Ask students to make sentences with the words they are given. Help where needed.
5. Have students leave word cards on tables and move one step to the left or right to find a different partner and two more words to practice.
6. Continue changing partners until all students are back to their original position.

Game 2: Zeros and Crosses

1. Decide (or have students decide) on nine words that need to be reviewed for active use.
2. Draw two zeros and crosses grids on the board, one with words and one without.
3. Have students form two teams. One team is zeros, the other crosses. Ask one team to choose a word and collaboratively make a sentence

with it. If it is correct, one student from that team puts their zero or cross on the blank grid.

4. Continue until the winning team makes a line (of Xs or 0s). (There are no extra or forfeited turns.)
5. Lastly, have students make sentences from words that have proved difficult during the game.

### Game 3: Same or Different

1. Pair off students, assigning one as A and the other B.
2. Give each an A or B sheet (see Appendix A).
3. Have students read out their word for each number, discuss its meaning, and write S (same) or D (different) beside each.
4. Discuss the words with the class and let students write down their partners' words. (Adapted from Nation, 1990)

### Game 4: Memory

1. Divide the class into groups of three or four.
2. Give each group a set of cards (see Appendix B). It is best to have at least twice as many different pairs of cards as there are students.
3. Place cards face down on a table, ask one student to pick up two cards, and read them out. If they form a pair, give the student another turn. If not, the next student has a turn. The student who has the most pairs when all pairs have been collected wins.

## Caveats and Options

1. Any combination of games can be used as appropriate to learners' needs, preferences, and the class situation.
2. In Game 2 (Zeros and Crosses), it is essential that the sentences passed have no grammatical, collocational, or lexical inaccuracies in them. This make-or-break aspect of the game engenders great team-work and collaboration before the sentence is finally put to the test in front of the other team and teacher.
3. In Game 3 (Same or Different), there are often no definitive right or wrong answers. Students are encouraged to talk about the possible meanings of a word in various contexts and of the possible similarities and differences that exist between the two words.

## References and Further Reading

Game 3 adapted from Nation, I. S. P. (1990). *Language teaching techniques*. Wellington, New Zealand: Victoria University.

## Appendix A: Sample Same or Different Game Sheet

| Sheet A | Sheet B |
|---------|---------|
| 1. Electorate | 1. Constituency |
| 2. Jerk | 2. Scrounger |
| 3. Consider | 3. Believe |

## Appendix B: Sample Memory Game Cards

*Note: Card pairs can be either word and definition or word and sentence with the word missing.*

| | |
|---|---|
| Electorate (n) | An area in which all the people in it have the right to vote in an election |

| | |
|---|---|
| Jerk (n) | A person you think is stupid and ignorant—usually an offensive word |

| | |
|---|---|
| To consider (v) | To think about something carefully |

| | |
|---|---|
| Electorate (n) | What _____ are you in? |

| | |
|---|---|
| Jerk (n) | He's a real _____. |

| | |
|---|---|
| To consider (v) | He wanted to _____ it first. |

## Contributor

*Linda Miles teaches in the Languages Unit of Otago Polytechnic in Dunedin, New Zealand. She teaches ESOL and Indonesian language and has lived and taught in Indonesia.*

# Sorry to Interrupt You, But . . .

**Levels**
High intermediate +

**Types**
General English course
emphasizing
communicative activities

**Aims**
Interrupt a conversation
politely and express
disagreement

**Class Time**
20–30 minutes

**Preparation Time**
15 minutes

**Resources**
Sentence strips

S tudents need to express themselves using real language. They do better when they have to perform a credible role, especially when they have to take on a humorous role and defend their point of view.

## Procedure

1. Post an announcement about a coming event on inventions on the chalkboard (see Appendix A). Tell your students that this is a real forum and that there will be real prizes for the winners (e.g., candy bars, chocolates, pencils).
2. Have the students form a circle, so that they can all see each other. Hand each one of them a sentence strip (see Appendix B), asking them not to show the part that explains their invention. They should show the other side to their classmates so that they can see some of the options they have in order to interrupt when necessary.
3. Invite them to explain their inventions one by one very briefly. After the last student has finished, have the first one start explaining the advantages of his or her invention and why he or she should be the winner. From that moment on, anybody can interrupt and explain his or her own invention and the reasons he or she should win.
4. Act as a moderator to ensure that the debate is lively. Try to involve all the participants.

## Caveats and Options

1. If you have a large number of students, pair them off. Seven individuals or seven pairs is a good number to practice this activity. The rest of the students may act as judges (deciding who the winner is after listening to the debate) or as the audience, asking the scientists questions about their inventions.

## Appendix A: Announcement

The chart of the diagram that you are going to have on the chalkboard might look like this:

> 1st International Forum of
> Superinventions
>
> Date
>
> Your school and classroom number
> Your city

## Appendix B: Sentence Strips

1. The sentence strips should be 11 inches long. On one side, write one of the following polite ways to interrupt:

   *Sorry to interrupt you, but . . . .*

   *That is really interesting, but . . . .*

   *Excuse me, but . . . .*

   *That sounds exciting, but . . . .*

   and any others that you consider appropriate. These expressions should be written in letters large enough so that the rest of the participants can see them and use them when they decide to make their points.

2. On the other side of the sentence strip, describe humorous inventions for your students to defend as their own. Make them as crazy as possible. For example:
   - You have just invented a chocolate bar vending machine that reminds its customers how fat they are before they buy its products.
   - You have just invented an uncomfortable chair for undesired guests.
   - You have invented a device that activates the door bell when somebody in your family has been using the telephone for more than 20 minutes.
   - You have just invented a special buffet detector that can locate any buffet in a 5-mile radius.

Example of a Completed Sentence Strip

On one side:

> You have just invented an uncomfortable chair for undesired guests.

and, on the other side,

> That sounds really interesting, but . . .

**Contributor**

*Francisco Ramos is a bilingual teacher working for the Los Angeles Unified School District, in California, in the United States.*

# Encouraging Formal Speech-Making

**Levels**
Intermediate

**Types**
Speaking

**Aims**
Speak formally as a precursor to formal speech making or the presentation of a seminar

**Class Time**
30 minutes +

**Preparation Time**
10 minutes (initially)

**Resources**
Several square pieces of cardboard with topics written on them
Paper bag or envelope to hold the topic cards

This activity is an enjoyable way to introduce formal speech-making in an ESOL classroom. By sharing preparation for the speeches, learners have the opportunity to practice formal speech-making.

## Procedure

1. Pair off students.
2. Have each pair pick a topic out of the bag or envelope of topics (e.g., immigration, the differences between males and females, love, a film to see, a book to read, learning a language, employment).
3. Have the students work on the topic together for 5 minutes. This includes dividing up the topic into two parts so that each part of a pair will speak about a different aspect of the topic.
4. Ask each pair to form a group with another pair and to present their shared, prepared talk to another pair. Each person, therefore, speaks in front of a partner and in front of two other people (a group of three).
5. Have each person speak for 2 minutes.
6. Each pair can deliver the same speech to another pair and vice versa.

## Caveats and Options

1. If you build up a resource paper bag of topics, this activity can lead to learners preparing their own talks and speaking independently to a group of four, and then gradually to half the class, and finally to the whole class.
2. The activity can be run as a modification of a 4-3-2 activity with each person in a pair reducing the time they take to deliver their speech

each time they deliver it to new people. Therefore, for each person, the length of the first delivery will be 2 minutes, the next, $1\frac{1}{2}$ minutes, and the last 1 minute.

3. This speaking activity can have a writing outcome if desired.

## Contributor

*Nikhat Shameem is a lecturer in the Institute of Language Teaching and Learning at the University of Auckland, in New Zealand.*

# Making Sentences Game

**Levels**
Beginning-intermediate

**Types**
General English

**Aims**
Review and use
vocabulary
Have fun while learning

**Class Time**
30–40 minutes

**Preparation Time**
None

**Resources**
Whiteboard
Whiteboard pens and
eraser

Reviewing vocabulary in context often requires teachers to think up a range of situations. An alternative is for students to think them up.

## Procedure

1. Remind the students of the vocabulary to be reviewed. List the words on one corner of the whiteboard.
2. Divide the class into groups, with a maximum of eight students per group.
3. Divide the white board into equal sections according to the number of groups.
4. Instruct students to line up in front of their part of the whiteboard. Give each group a whiteboard pen. Explain the rules for the game (see below).

Rules:

- Students have 15 minutes to write as many sentences that they can. These can be statements or questions. The group that makes the most correct sentences is the winner.
- Each sentence must contain one word from the vocabulary list.
- The first student writes a word on the board. It can be any word from the vocabulary list. This student then goes to the end of the queue. The second student in the queue comes up to add an appropriate word immediately either in front or behind this first word, then goes to the back of the queue. The third student adds another word either in front or behind these two words, then goes to the back of the queue and so on.

- Each new word added must be grammatically correct in relation to all the words written by the previous people in the group.
- The person who is in the queue immediately after the one who has just finished the previous sentence starts the new sentence for that group.
- This process is repeated until the time allowed is up.

5. Have students return to their seats.
6. Go through the sentences. Elicit corrections from the students themselves, when possible. Count the numbers of correct sentences for each group. Announce the winner.

## Caveats and Options

1. The game can be made easier for lower levels by allowing students to add a word when they can think of one instead of waiting for their turn. Make sure different students have a chance to start a new sentence.

## Contributor

*Trinh Thi Sao teaches in the School of Languages at Auckland Institute of Technology, New Zealand. She has taught ESL and Vietnamese.*

# Part VII: Nonverbal Stimuli

*Catering Ramos at Northern Virginia Community College, Alexandria, Virginia USA.*

# Introduction

If you enjoy using music, videos, pictures, or real-life objects to stimulate the class, you will find ideas here. Although most contributors take it for granted that teachers will provide all these materials, involving students in collecting them increases their commitment to the lesson planning. Some of the materials suggested can be part of a collection stored and shared by several teachers.

# Hit Parade

**Levels**
Intermediate +

**Types**
General English

**Aims**
Express opinions, likes,
and dislikes
Compare cultures
through music
Class Time
30–45 minutes

**Preparation Time**
Minimal

**Resources**
Audiotape or CD player
Three or four of your
favorite songs in English
on audiotape or CD
One favorite song from
the student's culture on
audiotape or CD

Music in the language class is a way of finding out about preferences of students from different cultures. It helps students relax and think.

## Procedure

1. Give students a brief introductory statement about music and culture. Tell them you are going to play part of one of your favorite songs.
2. First summarize the story line of the song and then play a short (1 minute) clip.
3. Have students rate the song on a scale of 1 to 10 (use Olympic style voting cards if you think it would be appropriate).
4. Finally, ask the students to bring a sample of their favorite song (melody and lyrics) for the next class period. Tell them they need to think about the story line of the song and encourage them to select a song that they consider typical for their age group in their culture.
5. Have students provide a synopsis of the story line in English.
6. Ask the class to rate the songs and discuss cultural values (relationships, feelings) that appear in the song. Raters should be prepared to justify their ratings; that is, they should give valid explanations for low ratings in order not to offend classmates.

## Caveats and Options

1. This activity can be used without rating the songs (i.e., only a discussion of values, symbols, and relationships). If you use ratings, you might opt for *I loved it, I liked it, It was okay*, and so on, so as not to offend students.
2. A written reaction (perhaps a newspaper critics' column) would be an interesting follow-up or journal activity.

*Dennis Bricault is director of ESL Programs and instructor in Spanish at North Park College, Chicago, in the United States.*

# Contributor

# Street Signs

**Levels**
Beginning (especially
students who do not
use the Roman
alphabet)

**Types**
Community class

**Aims**
Relate signs to services
Become familiar with a
new neighborhood

**Class Time**
5–10 minutes

**Preparation Time**
None, if you are familiar
with the neighborhood

**Resources**
Community

The world around them gives students many example of language that can remain a mystery. This activity tries to resolve the problem.

## Procedure

1. Draw a few signs on the board that students will recognize from their neighborhood (e.g., *Joe's Restaurant*). Ask a few questions, such as, *What is this? What does it say?* and *Where is it?* Then ask students about other stores and signs in the area. Have a few students write examples of signs on the board. Check for spelling, and help students with proper names.
2. For homework, tell students to wander around their neighborhoods and record 10 signs.
3. The next day, ask students to write on the board one or two examples of signs they found. The class can help with spelling and sense-making.

## Caveats and Options

1. You could divide the class into groups and ask each group to find 10 examples of a particular type of sign, for example: traffic, restaurants, clothing, shoes, furniture, or public announcements.
2. This activity could lead in many directions: role plays; what kinds of services each sign suggests (e.g., *What happens in a barber shop?*, *What can you buy at a drugstore?*); idiomatic expressions for more advanced students (e.g., a hair stylist's shop called *Curl Up and Dye*); or students could develop a local shopping/tour guide by designing a map.

3. I have used this activity in our very ethnically diverse neighborhood by asking students to find examples of store names in different languages (e.g., Korean, Chinese, Thai, Greek, Persian), which I use to lead into a topic on immigration.

## Contributor

*Dennis Bricault is director of ESL Programs at North Park College, Chicago, in the United States. He teaches structure, reading, and beginning Spanish.*

# Put the Piano Here

**Levels**
Beginning

**Types**
Twice weekly classes for
new immigrants

**Aims**
Practice giving
instructions and making
requests

**Class Time**
40 minutes

**Preparation Time**
30 minutes

**Resources**
Handout
Pictures of household
furniture and appliances
cut from old magazines
or advertising flyers

New immigrants often have to wait months for the arrival of their belongings. This activity prepares them with basic skills to instruct movers unloading their belongings.

## Procedure

1. Divide class into groups of two or four.
2. Give each group a handout of a house plan and some pictures of household furniture and appliances.
3. Ask students to imagine that their housepack has arrived and the movers are at the door.
4. Have students take turns at being the homeowner and the mover. Groups of four may have two homeowners (e.g., husband and wife) and two movers working at the same time, but everyone should have a turn at being the homeowner.
5. Have the movers start by holding up a picture and asking, "Where would you like this?" The homeowners must instruct the movers to put the furniture or appliance in a particular place in the house (based on the plan provided).

## Caveats and Options

1. This activity should be used in conjunction with or following lessons on giving instructions and or making requests.
2. Students should have prior knowledge of the names of rooms, furniture, and appliances in a typical modern home. However, some unusual items may make good conversation.

# Appendix:
# Sample
# House Plan

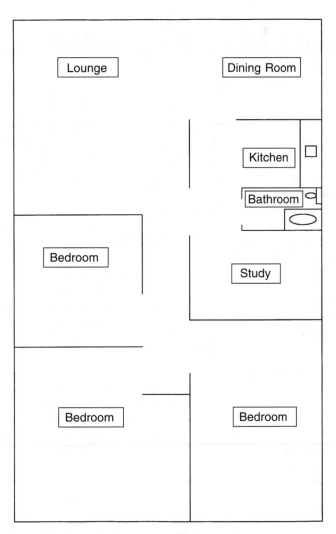

# Contributor

*Hazel Chan tutors at the University of Auckland, New Zealand, where she recently completed a Diploma in English Language Teaching. She has taught English as a second and foreign language in Singapore and New Zealand.*

# Using Pictures and Games

**Levels**
Low intermediate +

**Types**
Revolving admissions in
adult community
education setting

**Aims**
Review a particular
grammar structure using a
series of pictures from any
textbook with a story line
Create and roleplay dia-
logues based on a scene

**Class Time**
50 minutes

**Preparation Time**
1 hour

**Resources**
Transparencies of textbook
pictures containing
objective terminology
Overhead projector (OHP)
Picture worksheet for
labeling
Picture and text cloze
worksheets
Jigsaw picture and question
mark cards
Picture card(s) with several
characters for dialogue and
roleplay activities

Students attending community classes are usually looking for daily survival language skills. The following activities, based on daily occurrences, are used to get students with different levels of proficiency to practice the same vocabulary and skills at each of their levels.

## Procedure

1. Tell the students the topic of the lesson (e.g., automobiles and accidents) and explain to them that they are first going to do a whole-class activities and then work in groups.
2. Give low intermediate-level students a worksheet with the pictures or drawings to label for that lesson. This worksheet can later be used to help students complete other activities and to study.
3. Put the pictures on the OHP one at a time.
4. Ask students to name all of the objects they see in the pictures. If there is more than one word to describe an object, see if the students know them (e.g., *automobile: auto, car, vehicle*).
5. Label all the objects in the pictures on the transparencies for the low intermediate-level students to copy.
6. Divide the class into groups according to their level of proficiency. Assign roles to each of the students in the group (e.g., timekeeper, scribe, speaker).
7. Give low intermediate group(s) the vocabulary cloze exercise worksheet that you have prepared. Have the students complete the worksheet individually and then discuss their answers. If they are practicing a particular verb tense, give them that cloze worksheet instead. They can complete both or rewrite the vocabulary cloze using the verb tense that you want them to review.

8. Give the high intermediate-level group(s) the jigsaw picture with one or two question mark cards. Have them put the pictures in order. Have each group write a short paragraph for each of the pictures, making sure to use the verb tense that is being studied or reviewed and the correct connectives to give continuity to the story.

9. Give the advanced-level group(s) the picture with several characters. Have them imagine the dialogue taking place. The perspective to take can be assigned (e.g., *You just witnessed an accident and the police are questioning you,* or *You were just involved in an accident and the police are questioning you*) or free. Once they have finished creating their dialogues, have the group(s) roleplay them for the rest of the class.

## Caveats and Options

1. Instead of using picture stories you can also use comic strips with the dialogues deleted. You can also use these to have the students practice writing dialogues.

2. For whole-class oral descriptions, you can prepare some questions to ask in case students need prodding but make sure to use some of the objective terms in the questions. For example:
   ● What do you see in this picture?
   ● Which automobile is on the left side of the road?
   ● Which auto is in the right lane?

3. One variation for high intermediate- or advanced-level students is to set the example on how to ask the questions about what is contained in the picture and then let the students devise and ask their own questions while you monitor the structure of the questions and write them on the board.

4. This activity is also for high intermediate- and advanced-level students and can be done as a whole class or in smaller groups. Have a student pick a picture and orally describe what is in the picture. The other groups of students have all the pictures spread out in front of them. They listen to the description and wait until the student is finished. At that time they get 30 seconds to choose a picture and raise it for the rest of the class to see. The person who selects the correct picture first gets to describe the next one. If the students are working in

groups, the group that gets the correct picture first selects a representative to describe the next picture.

5. If you are using cartoon or comic strips that only have two or three pictures, have each student write a paragraph for a picture and as a group they have to join them together.

## References and Further Reading

Wright, A. (1984). *1000 pictures for teachers to copy*. New York: Longman Addison Wesley.

Wright, A. (1989). *Pictures for language learning*. Cambridge: Cambridge University Press.

Wright, A. (1990). *Visual materials for the language teacher*. New York: Longman.

## Contributor

*Lisa A. Hima is a curriculum project officer at an English language center in San Antonio, Texas, in the United States. She has been an adult education ESL teacher for 20 years in the United States, Mexico, and Japan.*

# *Anne of Green Gables* Gets Their Attention

**Levels**
Any

**Types**
University

**Aims**
Improve class
participation and
motivation
Build vocabulary
Improve listening and
speaking

**Class Time**
1–1½ hours for
approximately 12–15
weeks

**Preparation Time**
1–1½ hours per class

**Resources**
Video of *Anne of Green
Gables* (Parts 1 and 2)

**B**ecause *Anne of Green Gables* is a well known and popular story in Japan, the video may make a good basis for a variety of classroom activities there and elsewhere.

## Procedure

1. Give the students a vocabulary exercise (e.g., matching exercise).
2. Practice pronunciation.
3. Have students complete the handout for homework so that they are familiar with the vocabulary for the following week.
4. Go over the assigned vocabulary exercise. Have students write the matching words and phrases on the board. Go over it one more time before watching the video.
5. Give students a sequencing exercise.
6. Ask individual students to read a sentence from their handout giving the class the opportunity to ask about vocabulary they don't understand. Use an example from the story to explain vocabulary items.
7. Have students put these sentences in order while or after they watch the video.
8. Play about 20 minutes of the video. (The video is divided into 20-minute segments.)
9. When they finish watching the video, ask for the order of events in the handout.
10. Hand out a new vocabulary exercise for the following week.

## Caveats and Options

1. There is a lot of vocabulary for students to learn, so choose vocabulary judiciously. Some of the language in *Anne of Green Gables* is old-fashioned.

2. You can have students choose an incident from the story, write a short introduction and the dialogue, and present a short skit. Students can also make up discussion questions to go with their skit.

3. Students can give each other dictations. Put students into two groups and divide the vocabulary list into two columns, A and B. Give one group Column A vocabulary and the other Column B. Have students take turns dictating to each other. This gives them more practice with the vocabulary and the opportunity to practice helpful classroom language such as, *How do you spell _____? Please repeat that.*

4. Once students are comfortable with each other and the weekly format has been established, assign a section of the video (about 20 minutes) to a group of students. They can make up the vocabulary exercise, write the sequencing activity for the following week, or make up their own exercises and activities. They might even want to present a unit to the class.

5. Students can test each other on vocabulary. Follow Murphey's (1994/1995) suggestions for setting up a peer testing activity that maximizes students' use of real language. It is very helpful for them to be able to use examples from the story to explain their vocabulary rather than simply giving a one-word equivalent for each vocabulary item.

6. You can use other film versions of books that interest the class.

## References and Further Reading

Murphey, T. (1994/1995, Winter). Tests: Learning through negotiated interaction. *TESOL Journal*, pp. 12–16.

## Contributor

*Moira Izatt is currently teaching English Conversation in Japan. In Canada, she taught ESL and wrote educational materials. She is interested in learner motivation, learner-centered teaching, and learner-made materials.*

# Learning Proverbs Through Pictures

**Levels**
Advanced

**Types**
General English

**Aims**
Understand the meaning
of selected proverbs and
use them appropriately
in context

**Class Time**
10–15 minutes

**Preparation Time**
Minimal

**Resources**
Overhead transparency
with illustration of
proverb
Overhead projector
(OHP)

Explanations of proverbs in ESOL classes too often start from an explanation of the literal meaning together with a visual that focuses on illustrating the words literally. This can confuse learners and prevent them from understanding the metaphorical meaning and the application of the proverb in other contexts, especially when the words are obscure and the context culturally specific. If students are introduced to the concept first, then the idea of the proverb can be conveyed and appropriate contexts explored.

## Procedure

1. Display the picture of the proverb on the OHP.
2. Elicit information from the class about the content of the picture. For example:
   - *What are the people in the picture doing?* (Working, picking apples.)
   - *Why is more than one person doing this work?* (Work gets done more quickly, work is easier.)
   - *They are all helping each other. What is another expression for offering to help someone?* (Lend a hand.)
   - *So we can say lots of people helping makes the work easier. There's a proverb to express this idea: Many hands make light work.*
3. Have students think of a different example or story from experience to illustrate the proverb and discuss these examples in pairs.

## Caveats and Options

1. Students may enjoy making comparisons with proverbs of similar meaning in their own language, for example *to kill two birds with one stone* is *to hit two flies with one swipe* in German.

2. Students should be encouraged to write out their example stories without using the proverb. The stories can be distributed around the class for students to read and identify the proverbs they illustrate.
3. The drawings can be passed around the class for students to discuss and identify the proverbs they illustrate.

## Appendix: Many Hands Make Light Work

## Contributors

*Alison Kirkness is a teacher of ESOL and a teacher educator. She works at the Auckland Institute of Technology, in New Zealand. She has also taught EFL in Germany. Margaret Norris (illustration) lives and works in Auckland, New Zealand.*

# I Don't Think That's Funny

**Levels**
High beginning

**Types**
Listening and speaking classes, particularly EFL classes

**Aims**
Practice accurate, detailed description
Listen closely
Achieve a consensus through speaking and listening
Gain an understanding of Western concepts of humor

**Class Time**
5–10 minutes

**Preparation Time**
5 minutes

**Resources**
Comic strip, photocopied, mounted on card, and cut into frames

## Contributor

The interpretation of humor is culture specific. With careful choice of examples, this task can show students some differences from one culture to another.

## Procedure

1. Divide the class into groups so that the size of each group corresponds to the number of the frames in the comic strip.
2. Explain that every student will have one frame to describe to their group without showing the frame to anyone else. Warn that they may have to describe their picture more than once. Explain that, through listening, they must work out the correct order of the frames.
3. Distribute the comic strip frames and let the students begin.
4. Have the students place their frames face up in the order they think is correct, once the group has agreed on an order. After this, allow them to correct any mistakes they find once they can see all the frames.
5. Be prepared to explain the humor of the comic strip.

## Caveats and Options

1. The best strips to choose are usually those with a minimum of words and simple language rather than slang or unusual contractions.
2. A particular idea, such as the nature of a pun, may be introduced or reinforced through this activity.
3. Be aware that what may be an appropriate subject for humor in one culture may in fact be offensive in another. Exercise common sense.

*John Macalister is establishing an English language program at the Institute of Technology of Cambodia, Phnom Penh.*

# Cleansing the Gates of Perception

**Levels**
Intermediate +

**Types**
Private language schools

**Aims**
Prepare for an evening lesson by relaxing and stimulating creativity

**Class Time**
10 minutes

**Preparation Time**
1 hour

**Resources**
Music audiotape
Five pictures

Many working adults following English language courses are obliged to attend evening classes. These students often arrive at class tired and tense after a hard day of work. They may find it difficult to relax and concentrate on the lesson. It is important that adult working students get into a more relaxed and receptive state of mind before the lesson proper begins. The following activity stimulates the senses in a pleasant, interesting, and nondemanding way. It acts as a creative and imaginative transition between the working day and the language lesson.

## Procedure

1. Play an audiotape of three different and contrasting kinds of music, for example: a moody jazz piece, a Gregorian Chant, and some evocative Indian sitar music.
2. Display five pictures either on the board, around the room, or on an overhead projector. The pictures should be large enough for all students to see clearly. The pictures should be varied and as different from each other as possible, for example: a nighttime cityscape, a camel train crossing the desert, an eagle in flight, a mountain, and the Mona Lisa.
3. Ask students to listen to the music and, as they are listening, to match each of the three pieces of music with one of the pictures. Tell students that the matching is a matter of personal choice. There is no right or wrong answer. Instruct students not to write anything down.
4. Play the first piece of music again and ask students to share with the person sitting next to them which picture the music evoked for them. Repeat this procedure for the other two musical extracts. You may want to tell the class which picture the music evoked for you and give some reasons. Invite students to do the same.

## Caveats and Options

1. You may ask the students to decide which musical extract they liked best and to share this with the person sitting next to them.
2. You can substitute plain colors for the pictures, for example, different squares of green, red, gold, black, and yellow cardboard. The students then have to match the music with the color.
3. You can substitute shapes for the pictures, for example, circles, stars, squares, pyramids, and oblongs. The students then have to match the music with the shapes.

## Contributor

*Dino Mahoney is associate professor in the English Department of the City University of Hong Kong. He has also taught in England, Greece, and the United Arab Emirates.*

# Tell Me a Story

**Levels**
High intermediate

**Types**
Private language school;
general language class

**Aims**
Create a cooperative
story recycling
adjective/adverb
combinations, past
tenses, and linking
words

**Class Time**
50–60 minutes

**Preparation Time**
10 minutes

**Resources**
Picture prompts
Board outline

This activity provides a meaningful context for the integration of several pieces of language and provides a cooperative setting for the same. The task itself is controlled, and this is important for the management of a diverse but functionally related body of text.

## Procedure

1. Begin by reviewing linking expressions for time (e.g., *as soon as, while*) and other functions (e.g., *since, therefore, too*). Do this with a variety of sentence starters and an oral or written response. Include a broad sample of past tenses (past simple, past continuous, past perfect simple, and past perfect continuous) in these and check tense and aspect coordination.

2. Show three distantly related pictures to pairs of students (or groups of three) and ask them to imagine a likely story line connecting them. While they are doing this, put up on the board the outline (see Appendix) of the story framework and elements you want them to use.

3. Ask them to begin working together on their story incorporating the language you have highlighted. Have each student contribute equally and monitor each other for spelling and grammar.

## Caveats and Options

1. The activity presupposes previous study of past tenses, linking words, and adjective/adverb combinations.

2. If possible, have students compose their story on a word processor, so that on-the-spot corrections and monitoring are made easier. The final product can go into the school magazine.

3. This exercise is particularly useful for students whose written expression is limited.

## References and Further Reading

Hadfield, C., & Hadfield, J. (1990). *Writing games.* Surrey, England: Nelson.

**Appendix: Story Framework and Elements**

Linking Words

Time: *as soon as, until, before, while, after, as, by the time, since*
Logical connectors: *because, although, however, so, as well as, as, too, therefore*

Past Tenses

Past simple: to talk about actions and situations completed in a definite time in the past
Past continuous: to talk about a particular action or event in progress when another event took place (past simple)
Past Perfect Simple: to talk about events that happened before a specific time in the past (past tense)
Past Perfect Continuous: to talk about a long period of time in the past before another specific time in the past (past simple)

Adverbs of degree (to modify adjectives)

*extremely, rather, incredibly, quite, really, a bit, fairly*

**Contributor**

*Gavin Melles teaches at a private language school in Auckland, New Zealand. He has taught foreign languages and EFL at different levels in New Zealand and overseas. He is currently completing a DPhil (linguistics) at Waikato University.*

# Talking About Gifts

**Levels**
Intermediate

**Types**
Conversation classes

**Aims**
Practice speaking skills
Promote friendship
through gift-giving

**Class Time**
1–2 hours, depending
on number of students
in a class

**Preparation Time**
1–2 hours

**Resources**
Catalogues showing
some unusual gifts (e.g.,
a letter opener, a
musical timer)
Scissors, envelopes,
color markers
Holiday music tape
Handout

A great many natural talks can be generated by asking students to share with one another their private experiences and personal opinions about something simple and practical, such as gifts.

## Procedure

1. Start with a "show and tell" of a gift you have recently received to encourage students to talk about their own gifts.
2. Hand out the list (see Appendix) and ask students to practice reading it several times until they can use the expressions in their own sentences freely.
3. Hand out catalogues so that students can choose gifts for themselves and then cut the pictures out. Ask them not to tell anyone what they have chosen.
4. Tell students to find a partner and choose gifts for each other. Ask them to exchange gifts and explain reasons for their choices.
5. Ask the finished pairs to join another pair and select gifts for the rest of the class. Tell them to put the cut-out pictures of gifts in separate envelopes, one for each student and address the envelopes, for example:

> 12/20/96
> To: Ms Peiya Gu
> Best Wishes From
> Group 3

6. Turn on lively music. Ask each student to take a few envelopes with them and let the whole class walk about giving gifts to their classmates.

**Caveats and Options**

1. This activity is best done before holidays, for example Christmas and New Year. Students may enjoy bringing in real gifts next day and sharing their stories about these gifts, followed by continued talks about various cultural implications of gifts and giving in later classes.

**References and Further Reading**

Nolasco, R., & Arthur, L. (1990). *Conversation.* Oxford: Oxford University Press.

Brown, G., & Yule, G. (1983). *Teaching the spoken language.* Cambridge: Cambridge University Press.

## Appendix: List of Useful Expressions and Their Functions

1. The most recent gift I have received is . . . (describing)
2. I got that (from whom, when, where, how, why) . . .
3. I wish I could have a/an/some . . . (expressing a future intention)
4. I have selected . . . for myself/you because . . . (explaining)
5. I suggest we give . . . a/an/some . . . because . . . (giving one's opinion)
6. This is for you. I hope you like it. We thought you could use it for/ when . . . (giving a gift)
7. Thank you! It's beautiful/terrific/. . . It's just what I wanted/needed. I really love/like/need it. (accepting a gift and giving thanks)
8. You're welcome. I'm glad you like it. (accepting thanks)

**Contributor**

*Peiya Gu teaches at Suzhou University in China. Previously she taught ESL to adult immigrants in New York while studying at Teachers College, Columbia University in the United States.*

# Who Said That?

**Levels**
High beginning +

**Types**
One-to-one tutoring

**Aims**
Understand common idioms

**Class Time**
10 minutes

**Preparation Time**
20 minutes

**Resources**
List of common expressions
Series of pictures to match the utterances

English is full of idioms that are used in quite specific situations. Pictures are one way of making clear the meaning of idioms.

## Procedure

1. Choose pictures to illustrate common expressions. Display the pictures and have the student look at them as you read one of the expressions.
2. Ask the student to point at the appropriate picture.
3. Reverse roles.

## Caveats and Options

1. Ask the student to bring along examples of short, idiomatic utterances he has heard so that you can explain them.

## Appendix: Sample Expressions

Here are samples, with the pictures described in brackets.

1. Is that the lot? (Supermarket checkout)
2. Well, I mustn't hold you up. (Person on telephone)
3. You wouldn't have 50 cents would you? (person at parking meter)
4. Fill 'er up? (petrol pump attendant)
5. Can I check the oil? (petrol pump attendant)
6. What time do you make it? (person looking at watch)

## Contributor

*Margaret Richards has taught English to children and adults in Portugal. She is currently working as a volunteer home tutor in Auckland, New Zealand.*

# Who, Why, What, When?

**Levels**
High beginning

**Types**
One-to-one tutoring

**Aims**
Practice recognizing and remembering the difference between the English interrogatives

**Class Time**
5 minutes

**Preparation Time**
Minimal

**Resources**
Video recording of a television program
Remote control

One-to-one teaching can become boring for both student and tutors. Here is an idea for livening up the content by selecting points of interest for a TV program.

## Procedure

1. Agree on a program that both you and your student want to watch. Videotape the program (or have your student do it).
2. Take turns with your student holding the remote control and deciding when to press pause.
3. When you have stopped the program, fire a question at the student, varying the interrogative words from question to question (e.g., *who, what, why*). When your student has the remote, have him ask you questions.

## Caveats and Options

1. The student could prepare the questions beforehand and write them down.

## Contributor

*Margaret Richards has taught English to children and adults in Portugal. She is currently working as a volunteer home tutor in Auckland, New Zealand.*

# The Bank Stops Here

**Levels**
Low intermediate

**Types**
Any

**Aims**
Utilize visual and kines-
thetic modes of learning
Practice prepositions of
location

**Class Time**
20–30 minutes

**Preparation Time**
4 hours

**Resources**
Textbook section on prep-
ositions of location
Large version of a scene
in a textbook and similar
buildings on separate
small pieces of paper
Large drawing of the same
scene as the textbook on
posterboard or a real one
from the neighborhood
with streets and blocks
drawn in with marker
Pictures of various types
of buildings (drawn or
photocopied) on small
pieces of paper or cards

Classes of low intermediate students can benefit from using one set of visual resources in several ways. Here they make their own decisions about where to place items on a map.

## Procedure

1. Put students in pairs or small groups to practice the patterns from the book or additional ones. For example, one student can give directions (*Put the bank next to the drugstore*) and another student can place the appropriate building where directed.
2. Have students arrange their scene, then write sentences or a paragraph of description to be checked by you or other students. Conversely, students can arrange their scene to show comprehension of other students' descriptions.

## Caveats and Options

1. Students can make the scene board and the buildings themselves. Laminating all the pieces will make them useful longer.
2. Having several boards and pieces, either identical or not, will enable extensive pair practice.

# Appendix: Sample Pictures

# Contributors

*Lise Winer teaches in the TESOL and Applied Linguistics programs at Southern Illinois University, Carbondale, Illinois, in the United States. Dragana Golubovic (illustrations) is a student in Art and Design, Southern Illinois University, Carbondale.*

# You Can Be a Talk Show Guest

**Levels**
Advanced

**Types**
Listening and speaking

**Aims**
Improve conversational
English

**Class Time**
2 hours (using a 30-
minute talk show)

**Resources**
Audio- or videotape of
call-in talk show on a
current, worthwhile
topic

## Caveats and Options

## Contributors

In this activity, students use the conversations of real people calling into a talk show (TV or radio) to learn new vocabulary, practice using the new vocabulary correctly, and express their own feelings on a subject. If the students are sufficiently advanced, they may even simulate a follow-up show on the same topic or a slightly different topic.

## Procedure

1. Play the tape, having students note any words or phrases that are unfamiliar.
2. Have students find definitions for the unfamiliar words or discuss them in class.
3. Play the tape again if necessary and make sure that students understand the dialogue.
4. Have students write summaries of their comments and ideas on the topic.
5. Lead students in a discussion of the topic and encourage the use of new vocabulary.

1. Assign each class member one person from the tape to study closely. Then repeat the situation with class members playing the roles of the talk-show host and callers.
2. Identify a similar topic, have class members research the vocabulary and facts, and then direct class members to simulate a talk show with the new topic.

*Janet Winter teaches business communication at Central Missouri State University, in the United States. Esther Winter teaches English at Northwest Missouri State University, in the United States. Olga Boriskina teaches English at English Voronezh State University in Russia.*

# Part VIII: Task Instructions or Demonstrations

*Dae Wook No at Northern Virginia Community College, Alexandria, Virginia USA.*

# Introduction

In some parts of the world, teachers have to prepare lessons without access to photocopy machines or many resource books. In these cases, the teacher has to create interesting and varied lessons without the benefit of materials. The following activities can all be completed with minimal resources (which is not the same as saying without planning).

# Stretching the Point

**Levels**
Intermediate +

**Types**
English for further
study/academic
purposes courses

**Aims**
Understand the shape
and structure of a
formal talk in English
Organize and present
oral information
effectively and
confidently
Practice question
formation at short
notice

**Class Time**
22 minutes/student

**Preparation Time**
None

**Resources**
Video camera

In this activity, students learn how to develop a 5-minute talk by expanding a set of headings they have noted on the topic. They become more aware of the shape of an oral presentation in English and how to arrange the content of their talks to maximize their communicative effectiveness. The other students in the class are randomly called on to ask questions during each talk, which serves to keep everyone involved.

## Procedure

1. Discuss with students the concept of oral presentations and some of the situations in which they are used—at work, in study, and in the community. If students express doubt that they can sustain a talk for more than a couple of minutes, explain that through using a new approach called "stretching the point" they will find that they can in fact can do this.
2. Tell the students that they will each be asked to present a 5-minute talk on a topic of their choice.
3. Ask each student to note down the topic of their talk.
4. Draw up the schedule for the presentations.
5. Ask students to list approximately five headings under their topic, for example:

   Topic: Kangaroos
   Headings: physical description, distribution, breeding cycle, food, enemies

   Assign background work on the topic over the next days or over the weekend. Suggest to them also that they may like to assemble some material such as charts, maps, photographs, or models to support their talk.

6. Outline the technique: A student comes to the front of the class, announces the title of the talk, and writes on the board the headings under which the talk will be organized. (You can model the entire process.) You will then call on any one of the students in the audience to ask a question on the first heading (e.g., *Can you describe what kangaroos look like?*). Only when a question is correctly formulated can the presenter proceed to give information on it. It is desirable that more than one question be asked, and the questions should be ones that will enable the presenter to talk for a while rather than give a yes/no answer. Follow this procedure until all the headings are covered. You will want to videotape the presentation.

7. Watch the video and analyze each presenter's performance under headings such as:
   - organization of information
   - overall communicative effectiveness
   - effective use of supporting material.

**Caveats and Options**

1. In subsequent courses, use these videotaped talks as models.

## Contributor

*Stephanie Claire works for the New South Wales Adult Migrant English Service, in Australia. She is currently involved in the assessment of language gains within a competency-based curriculum.*

# Flower-Gathering Method for Composition

**Levels**
Advanced

**Types**
University

**Aims**
Exchange ideas with classmates for a composition topic
Learn different ways to approach a general topic

**Class Time**
45 minutes

**Preparation Time**
10 minutes

**Resources**
None

## Appendix: Sample Opening Sentences

## Contributor

Comparing cooperative group work with the metaphor of gathering flowers is one way of stressing the importance of everyone's contributions.

## Procedure

1. Divide the class into five groups of about six students each.
2. Announce the topic or opening sentence of the composition. Explain that as they work in groups they will be "gathering flowers" for a bouquet, which will be their own finished composition.
3. Have the students in each group work together to make their four best sentences ("flowers"). Give them about 15 minutes to do this.
4. Have the group leaders come to the board and write their sentences simultaneously to save time.
5. Have the students work individually at their own compositions, drawing on the 20 sentences and using connections and transitions taught in earlier classes.

## Caveats and Options

1. Give students the freedom to change the opening sentence as long as they keep to the same topic.

1. In studying English or any other language, we must master its grammar and have a rich vocabulary.
2. When I speak English, I only use English.
3. English is an international language.
4. Learn to think in English whenever you think alone.
5. To write a personal diary is one of the best ways of studying.

*Duong Bach Nhat teaches English in the English Department of Qui Nhon Teachers' College, Vietnam.*

# That's Not What I Said

**Levels**
Low intermediate

**Types**
Speaking and listening skills

**Aims**
Practice careful listening to a story
Practice retelling a story
Identify differences between versions of the same story
Gain an understanding of different cultures through sharing stories

**Class Time**
15–20 minutes

**Preparation Time**
None

**Resources**
None

When students have to listen and retell a story, they are practicing for many real-life tasks where listening for details is important.

## Procedure

1. Divide the class into two groups of equal size, Group A and Group B. Send Group B out of the room.

2. Tell a story to Group A. Write key words and draw pictures on the board as you narrate. Do not let students write anything down, however. Leave the words and pictures on the board when you have finished.

3. Bring in Group B. Tell each student in Group B to sit with a student in Group A. Explain that Group A heard a story that they are now going to tell Group B.

4. Ask students in Group A to retell the story to their partner. Move around the class to monitor and encourage students.

5. When Group A has finished telling the story, tell Group B to move to a different partner. Now ask Group B to retell the story they just heard from Group A.

6. Ask Group A if they heard the same story they heard earlier. Ask them to identify any differences.

7. Retell the story to the whole class, involving the students in this final retelling through questioning.

## Caveats and Options

1. The story chosen should not be too long nor too complicated. Legends are a fine source of suitable tales.

2. Some teachers may choose to extend this activity by asking the students to write the story. Some stories are also suitable to be developed into dramatic sketches.

## Contributor

*John Macalister is establishing an English language program for the Auckland Institute of Technology at the Institute of Technology of Cambodia, Phnom Penh.*

# What Do You Know About Me?

**Levels**
Intermediate +

**Types**
Weekly class

**Aims**
Become more familiar
with the teacher as a
person

**Class Time**
30 minutes

**Preparation Time**
None

**Resources**
None

The purpose of this activity is to demystify the role of the teacher and reveal the teacher as a person. Many students are curious about their teachers. When the teacher offers personal information, learners feel they are being treated as adults.

## Procedure

1. Have students work in pairs or groups to think of any questions they would like answered about you. (Depending on how brave you feel, you can allow complete freedom or establish some boundaries).
2. Identify a student with an outgoing personality and ask him or her to come to the front of the class.
3. Stand to one side.
4. Invite the class to ask the student their questions about you. Instruct the student to answer in the first person as if he or she were you. The student can answer however he or she wants. For questions where the answers are unknown, tell the student to guess the answer.
5. At the end of the question session, indicate the percentage of answers that were correct and tell the class that they should try to find out in any way they can which answers were correct and what the answers were to those answered falsely. The class has 1 month to do this. Repeat the activity after 4 weeks.

## Caveats and Options

1. You could try the same activity using students as the focus for the questions. That is, one student answers personal questions on behalf of another. The students may then be motivated to talk to each other after class to find out which questions were answered correctly.

## Contributors

*Lindsay Miller is assistant professor in the English Department at City University of Hong Kong. David Gardner is senior language instructor in the English Centre of the University of Hong Kong.*

# Childhood Memories

**Levels**
Intermediate

**Types**
Integrated skills class for recent immigrants

**Aims**
Speak and listen
Get to know other class members
Take notes

**Class Time**
20 minutes

**Preparation Time**
None

**Resources**
None

One of the resources in every class is memories of childhood. Talking about games is a good way of finding out about the countries represented in the group.

## Procedure

1. Pair off students.
2. Ask students to recall their favorite childhood game. Give them 2 minutes to think.
3. Tell students to share their memories of their favorite game with their partner. They should take notes with the purpose of reporting the information to the class.
4. After 10 minutes, have students describe to the class the favorite game of their partner.

## Contributor

*Holly Patrick is a graduate student at Georgia State University, in the United States.*

# Is the Price Right?

**Levels**
Intermediate

**Types**
Integrated skills class for
recent immigrants

**Aims**
Speak, listen, write
Practice numbers and
descriptive words
Learn prices of products
in the new country

**Class Time**
30 minutes

**Preparation Time**
5 minutes

**Resources**
Blank price tags
Markers

S tudents can be involved in bringing the resources for this exercise, which suggests an interesting way of practicing vocabulary.

## Procedure

1.  Have each student bring in three ordinary objects found in a grocery or drug store and their prices. Have students write a short description of the product.
2.  Divide the class into two groups: Team A and Team B. Ask students to put the prices of the items on price tags and give the products to you with the price tag and product description. Keep the products brought in by each team separate.
3.  Create two price tags with incorrect prices for each product.
4.  Start the game by choosing a product brought in by Team A with its three price tags (one correct, two incorrect). Ask that the person who brought in the product come up to the front of the class and describe the product, using the description he or she wrote. Team B must guess which price is the correct one. The teams take turns reading product descriptions and guessing prices. The winning team is the one that guesses the correct price of the products most often.

## Contributor

*Holly Patrick is a graduate student at Georgia State University, in the United States.*

# You Talk, I Write

**Levels**
Low intermediate

**Types**
One-to-one tutoring

**Aims**
Acquire language
needed to talk about
topics of interest
Boost confidence
Identify target structures
to learn

**Class Time**
30 minutes

**Preparation Time**
None

**Resources**
Pen and paper

## Appendix: Sample Dictation With Corrections

Using students' talk as the basis for their writing is a familiar approach in elementary schools. Here the teacher uses the students' ideas as the basis for language learning.

## Procedure

1. Ask the student what he wants to say to other people.
2. As the student talks, write exactly what he says leaving plenty of space between lines for changes.
3. Ask the student to read the dictated piece back to you. Suggest alternative ways of saying things. (See Appendix.)
4. Highlight a particular point of grammar that the student seems ready to learn about.
5. Give the student the two versions to use: one for his own study and one for talking with other people.

## Caveats and Options

1. Occasionally the order can be reversed. As you talk about yourself, the student writes down what you say in note form and then expands it into complete sentences with your assistance.

*Note: The teacher's draft of the original version follows with the suggestions in the lines between.*

After that I and my family went to car and came to city and we had dinner

       *to the car*                    *to the city*

216

in McDonald's. All the hamburger at McDonald's have New

    *all the hamburgers*      *are made from*

Zealand meat. And everywhere in world children like McDonald's. We went to car

    *in the world*      *to the car*

and go home.

    *went*

## Contributor

*Margaret Richards has taught English to children and adults in Portugal. She is currently working as a volunteer home tutor in Auckland, New Zealand.*

# Sharing Out the Jobs

**Levels**
Intermediate

**Types**
General English

**Aims**
Participate in speaking
activities
Ensure more even
participation among
group members during
speaking tasks

**Class Time**
Variable

**Preparation Time**
Very little

**Resources**
Pieces of colored
cardboard to make "job
cards"

Allocating students a "job," that is, a set responsibility and a set turn, is useful for encouraging reluctant speakers to participate in speaking activities. It is particularly useful when the learners all speak the same language, are reluctant to stand out from the group, and find it unnatural to speak English to each other. By allocating a student a job card with instructions to carry out a speaking task as part of a group activity, the teacher takes the burden of volunteering away from the student and requires the student to contribute to the group or class speaking activity. Learners are usually aware of their responsibility to their group and participate as required.

## Procedure

1. During group discussion, give each student a card with a particular question to answer or a statement to comment on.
2. For a controversial question, give each student a card with a particular job described on it. For example:
   - It is your job to disagree with the other speakers.
   - It is your job to agree with the other speakers.
   - It is your job to try to make the other speakers agree.
   - It is your job to summarize the discussion.
   - It is your job to report back to the class on the group discussion.
3. Use job cards to establish set turns of uninterrupted speaking. Hand each student in a group a card with an instruction on it. For example: *It is your job to speak for 2 minutes without stopping on the subject of . . . .*

218

4. When students give prepared oral presentations to the class, give other students job cards in advance. Job cards can have instructions such as:
- Introduce the speaker.
- Thank the speaker.
- Comment on an interesting aspect of the talk.
- Ask the speaker a question.

**Contributor**

*Moina Simcock teaches at the English Language Institute, Victoria University of Wellington, New Zealand.*

# Speaking Skills
# Confidence Builder

**Levels**
Beginning–intermediate

**Types**
Polytechnic; general
English

**Aims**
Establish rapport with
other students
Practice clarifying
information, and asking
and answering questions
Become more confident
speaking English

**Class Time**
30–40 minutes per talk

**Preparation Time**
None

**Resources**
One sheet of butcher
paper
Whiteboard, pen, eraser
Adhesive

Speaking to a group can be a frightening experience for second language learners. In this case, a 5-minute talk is long enough to say something, but not too long to run out of words.

## Procedure

1. Organize a talk schedule with the students. Negotiate with each student a suitable time to give a 5-minute talk. Allow only one talk per session or, if possible, one or two talks per week.
2. Write the agreed talk schedule on the sheet of butcher paper and put it on the wall. Have students write on the chart their chosen topic before their turn to talk. Be sure to schedule the first talk so that there is enough time for the student to prepare it.
3. Before each talk, instruct students to listen and ask for clarification of anything that is not clear to them during the talk. This could include asking the speaker to draw a picture or to write on the whiteboard words and phrases that are difficult for them to follow. Inform them that at the end of the talk they will be asked questions to check their understanding of the main points.
4. Sit the speaker in front of the class, then move to the back. Listen and note words, phrases, and sentences that caused misunderstanding for practice with the class later. Model the techniques of questioning and clarifying the first few times if students are unsure.
5. When the talk has finished, depending on the students' English ability, either ask questions to check understanding or ask one or two students at random to summarize the main points.
6. Go through linguistic items of common interest and usefulness with the whole class.

7. Some topics can lead to lively comparative discussion of similar experiences and new knowledge about one another's culture, family circumstances, work experience, individual ability, areas of interest, and so on.

**Caveats and Options**

1. Do not try this until you have created a supportive atmosphere among your students.
2. Do not force any student to do this activity. However, do ask them to participate in asking questions.
3. Use this activity only after lessons in clarification and questioning have been taught.
4. Building confidence and language competence is a continuous process. More language items should be included and practiced in later talks in the same schedule.

**Contributor**

*Trinh Thi Sao teaches in the School of Languages at Auckland Institute of Technology, New Zealand. She has taught English and Vietnamese.*

# Learning Exchange

**Levels**
Any

**Types**
Private language school

**Aims**
Develop oral fluency

**Class Time**
50 minutes or lunch hour

**Preparation Time**
20 minutes

**Resources**
Card, paper, glue, felt pen

In this activity, students operate as tutors to fellow students and teachers, teaching an activity they are skilled at. They gain a sense of worth and are highly motivated to acquire the vocabulary needed to explain their activity.

## Procedure

1. Prepare a poster advertising the time and place of the Language Learning Exchange. Suggest possible activities according to the students' talents (e.g., Chinese massage, Tai Chi, Spanish dancing, Japanese cooking). Have an accompanying sheet for students to sign headed:

   What do you want to learn? What are you able to teach?

2. Create a timetable for the exchange and match students and teachers.

## Contributor

*Deirdre Walsh teaches in the ESOL Department of St. Andrew's College, Christchurch, New Zealand. She has also worked in private language schools.*

# Getting Acquainted

**Levels**
Low intermediate

**Types**
General English

**Aims**
Develop fluency
Negotiate vocabulary

**Class Time**
40 minutes

**Preparation Time**
None

**Resources**
Chinese Zodiac
List comparison
vocabulary (e.g., *As ...
as a . . .*)

Students can develop fluency when asked to talk about familiar ideas. Animals have a different place in each culture, which makes this activity interesting in a class of varied nationalities.

## Procedure

1. Begin by eliciting the characteristics attributed to animals in various cultures. This may be done by:
   - Encouraging students from different backgrounds to talk about the zodiac (e.g., the Chinese lunar years), or
   - Getting students to supply sayings that relate to their culture with regard to animal characteristics (e.g., *as wise as an owl*).
2. Put students into groups of four. Ask each student to spend a few minutes thinking about the characteristics of an animal or creature they can strongly relate to. Ask them to describe the animal's attributed characteristics and say why these are similar to their own. An example such as the following can be given:

   I think I am like a cat. Cats are soft. They respond to kindness. They like to be comfortable, to have plenty of food, and a warm place to sleep. They are also quite independent and like to spend time alone. However, cats scratch if someone hurts or frightens them.

3. After each student has contributed to a whole-group conversation, saying as much or as little as they wish, have a spokesperson for each group give feedback by telling the class what each person said.

## Caveats and Options

1. This could be an exercise in reported speech, in which case the information will be given anonymously (e.g., "One student in our

group said he was like a dog because dogs are loyal friends and like company. Dogs will protect their friends in times of danger.")

2. Language points that could be frequently repeated are:
   - *as ... as a ...*
   - *similar to ...*
   - *on one hand ... ; on the other hand ...*
3. Groups could write a summary of the discussion in their group on newsprint. This could be displayed on the wall of the classroom.

## Contributor

*Denice Worthington currently teaches at the English Language Institute at Victoria University of Wellington, in New Zealand. She has also taught ESL in polytechnics and community classes.*

# Part IX: Other People

*Martha Zoraida García and Carla Ramos at Northern Virginia Community College, Alexandria, Virginia USA.*

# Introduction

One important resource in English-speaking countries is people in the wider community. These people speak and write in ways that are not controlled by a language specialist such as a teacher. Even in countries where English is not usually spoken, visitors can take part in class in various ways. In this section, teachers report ways they have guided their students in meaningful interaction with spoken and even written English.

# Visiting Seniors

**Levels**
Any

**Types**
Private language school

**Aims**
Develop conversation
skills with patient and
courteous listeners
Learn more about the
role of senior citizens in
the host country

**Class Time**
1 hour

**Preparation Time**
30 minutes

**Resources**
Senior citizens

## Caveats and Options

It is often difficult to find good conversation partners for students outside of the classroom, especially if they do not have a job or other extracurricular social activities. Typically, children and senior citizens are some of the easiest people for ESL students to converse with. Visiting a retirement home can be a delightful way to help remove the intimidation that many ESL students feel about talking with strangers.

## Procedure

1. Contact a local retirement home and arrange for your students to visit. We have found that participating in an afternoon social gathering like tea time is the easiest and most natural context for this visit.
2. Prepare your students for the visit by comparing the role of senior citizens in their cultures and yours. Talk about the advantages and disadvantages of old age, the challenges seniors face, and how they deal with these challenges. Go over a list of suitable discussion topics (e.g. career, grandchildren, early life, hobbies, retirement, travel, changes in their lifetimes).
3. On the day of your visit, try to arrange it so that your students are evenly spread out among the seniors. This works best if they can be arranged at small tables.
4. Circulate among the students as necessary to provide assistance.
5. Debrief students when you get back to class or on the next day.

1. No matter how hard you try, there will always be some combinations of students and seniors that do not work well. If either feel that they are being expected to do this out of obligation, genuine conversation may be difficult. This is part of learning how to communicate in a language and cannot be avoided.

2.  When this activity works, it works very well. Students that make an effort to talk with seniors often get invited back to visit again. Some of our students have even developed long-term friendships with the seniors they have met.

## Contributors

*Mark Dickens is a freelance writer, editor, and ESL teacher who lives in Victoria, British Columbia, Canada, where he most recently taught at Fields College International. Erica Hofmann is currently working on her PhD in Austin, Texas, in the United States. Before this, she taught ESL at Fields College International.*

# The Real Thing

**Levels**
Any

**Types**
Any

**Aims**
Extend fluency and
listening skills
Meet a range of native
speakers

**Class Time**
1 hour

**Preparation Time**
15 minutes

**Resources**
Volunteer native English
speakers
Question/discussion
guide on current
classroom topic/theme
Name tags

This activity is designed to simulate a social gathering where learners interact with native speakers, male and female, of all ages and from all walks of life. The teacher has the opportunity to observe students in a real conversational situation. The native speakers have the opportunity to meet and talk to a range of interesting students.

## Procedure

1. Allow native speakers 5 minutes to preview the question/discussion guide.
2. Calculate native speaker/student ratio. An ideal ratio is one speaker to three students.
3. Make up groups of different nationalities.
4. Assign one native speaker to each group.
5. Initiate discussion.
6. Rotate groups of learners.

## Caveats and Options

1. The success of the program relies heavily on the reliability of the native speakers. Encourage volunteers to commit themselves for a predetermined period (e.g., 4-6 weeks) and to contact their partners when scheduling conflicts occur.
2. Offer some awareness raising/training.
3. Allow time at the end of the session for feedback from volunteers.

4. The length of time spent with each native speaker may vary according to such things as
   - level of language
   - number of native speakers
   - total time available.

5. Volunteers could include home tutors, TESOL trainees, family members, and speakers related to specific topics (e.g., immigration officer and staff members).

6. Change location (e.g., meet at local Botanic Gardens or local school).

7. Regroup learners each rotation.

8. Vary discussion style/content; include questions, descriptions, and opinions.

9. Offer a more structured framework at lower levels.

10. Bring personal photos on the first day for introductions.

## Contributor

*Linda Gowing teaches ESOL at Otago Polytechnic, Dunedin, New Zealand.*

# Perfect Match

**Levels**
Intermediate +

**Types**
Language school on a
university campus

**Aims**
Speak fluently one-to-
one in an authentic
context

**Class Time**
1 hour (over two class
periods)

**Preparation Time**
2-4 hours

**Resources**
Students who speak a
range of languages
Application forms
Posters

Students often want to practice speaking in an authentic context. A communicative activity with native speakers can meet this need. The main difficulty in establishing and maintaining such an activity is in motivating native speaker involvement and commitment. A solution can be found in the language students on campus with a similar need to the ESL students, that is to practice productive skills in an authentic context with a native speaker.

## Procedure

1. Identify a source of students learning the L1(s) of students in your class, for example the Modern Languages Department. Promote this activity to the language students by liaising with their lecturers, visiting their classes, or producing a poster for display in classrooms and notice boards. Ask interested students to complete a registration form with details such as L1, L2, current course, hobbies or general interests, preferred partner characteristics, and how the student thinks the activity will help to improve the L2.
2. Introduce the activity to your class and generate student interest by emphasizing the importance of practicing conversation in an authentic context. Have your students complete a registration form too.
3. Match students in pairs, using the information on the registration forms.
4. Arrange for all the language students to attend your class to meet their partners. Place the matched students in pairs. Ask the students to introduce themselves to each other and to practice speaking in both the L1 and L2. Try to identify and resolve any compatibility problems. Outline guidelines. For example, you expect the pairs to meet at least

once a week for a minimum of 1 hour but preferably more frequently. Elicit topic ideas from the students. Emphasize that the students must spend equal time in L1 and L2.

5.  Monitor the progress of the pairs at regular intervals.

## Caveats and Options

1.  This communicative activity can require some time to establish but eventually the students take responsibility for it, developing independent learning skills.
2.  This activity could be adapted to a classroom context as a regular weekly activity or as an exchange between two monolingual groups such as a class of English speakers and a class of Italian speakers. It could also be adapted to an exchange in writing.
3.  Students could keep a log book of their meetings or record their conversation in L2 for learning awareness activities in class.

## Appendix: Sample Registration Form

Conversation Exchange Program

Registration Form

Date:

Name:

Please tick:  ☐ male  ☐ female

Address:

Telephone Number:

Course you are studying at Macquarie University:

Year/level of your course:

Your first language:

Language you wish to practice:

Preferred Partner Characteristics (e.g., male, female, interests, graduate, postgraduate, science or humanities, student):

How long will you be studying in Australia?

Why would you like to join the conversation exchange program?

## Contributor

*Giselle Kett has taught ESOL for 10 years in Australia and Japan. She is currently the Independent Learning Centre coordinator at the National Centre for English Language Teaching and Research, Macquarie University, in Sydney, Australia.*

# What Do You Want to Know?

**Levels**
Intermediate +

**Types**
Adults of a variety of ages and language backgrounds in an ESOL class for new settlers

**Aims**
Become familiar with the range of services available in the new country
Increase confidence in asking questions

**Class Time**
Two or three 45-minute lessons

**Preparation Time**
Time to make telephone arrangements

**Resources**
Visiting speaker

Listening to visiting speakers can create a passive environment for students. In this activity, students listen actively for specific answers to their own questions.

## Procedure

1. Agree on areas of life in the new country that students would like to know more about.
2. Have students formulate questions that they would like to ask a knowledgeable person.
3. Work together to make the questions clear.
4. Invite one speaker per day, supplying them with the questions beforehand.
5. Have students ask the questions orally (even though the speaker has seen them beforehand).
6. Be sure to have one student thank the speaker on behalf of the class.
7. After the speaker has left, talk about what they have learned as you write key words and phrases on the board.
8. Have students write down individually what they have learned making use of the key words and phrases written on the board.

## Caveats and Options

1. This activity can expand into three separate days or the questions can simply be planned orally on the day the speaker is coming.

## Contributor

*Marilyn Lewis has taught English to new immigrants in Auckland, New Zealand.*

# This Is My Brother

**Levels**
Beginning

**Types**
Beginners on-arrival
course in English and
orientation

**Aims**
Meet people in a new
country
Use minimal English for
genuine social contacts

**Class Time**
1 hour

**Preparation Time**
Enough time for
telephone calls

**Resources**
Visitors
Photographs
Atlases
Morning tea
Interpreter

The challenge to a teacher of absolute beginners is to help them feel as if they have a role to play socially. This activity allows them to be hosts as they meet new people.

## Procedure

1. Invite people of a range of ages and interests to come to class at morning tea time with photographs.
2. Practice beforehand offering tea and coffee using one word only and an interrogative intonation. (*Tea or coffee? Milk? Sugar?*)
3. Review two questions (*Who's this? Where's this?*).
4. On the day of the visit, have the class prepare tea and coffee. Arrange chairs informally.
5. Introduce visitors and students. As the drinks are served, have students and visitors communicate in basic English, exchanging information about people and places from photograph albums and the atlas. Have an interpreter available in case of difficulties.

## Contributor

*Marilyn Lewis has taught classes at the Refugee Resettlement Centre in Auckland, New Zealand.*

# Bring Some Language to Our Class

**Levels**
Intermediate +

**Types**
One-to-one teaching,
particularly in an L2
environment

**Aims**
Make use of language
heard outside class
sessions
Take responsibility for
the selection of
language materials and
the course of the
session

**Class Time**
20 minutes

**Preparation Time**
None

**Resources**
Language notebook
Glue
Index cards

In this activity, students bring some language from their experiences during the week (e.g., words, phrases, ads, a section of a newsletter) to the one-to-one session. This material forms the start of the session, is discussed and entered in a language notebook, and is then integrated with previous or current language work. The activity makes the students responsible for initiating the preliminary content of the session. It also encourages students to give attention to the target language on a daily basis, beyond the class session. By continuing to refer to and use the language that students bring, you show that what they choose is of value and that it is possible for them to learn from the wider L2 environment.

## Procedure

1. Ask students to bring to the language session three pieces of language that they have observed or met during the week. Have the students present these pieces of language one at a time (orally, on paper, or on a videotape). Students should be able to explain when and where the language was found and why it was chosen.
2. Ask the student about the language: *When did you find it? Where did you find it? What else did you notice? Why did you choose it? What do you think it means?*
3. Record together language from the discussion, for example: key words, observations, a mind map, a summarizing sentence, or typical uses of new words. Use a separate page in the language notebook for each of the three pieces of language.
4. Make connections wherever possible between this language and previous work in the language notebook. Also, whenever possible, incorporate the language notebook with other aspects of the lessons that you prepare.

5. Provide students with opportunities for repeated practice of the language that has been the focus of the session. (One idea is to put key words on cards with a sample sentence on the back for students to review.)
6. Keep a record for yourself of the language used in the session to assist with Steps 4 and 5 in future sessions.

## Caveats and Options

1. This activity requires you to respond creatively and imaginatively to the language brought by the student. Use the material in an interesting way, extend it, and make clear to the student which specific words, phrases, or structures they should remember and use.
2. Be careful not to get into the position of explaining the language to the student. Make sure what you say is part of a dialogue.
3. Be selective—there is no need to make exhaustive use of everything.
4. Occasionally some of the material the student presents may be difficult to work with—mention why this is so and move on.

## Contributor

*Cynthia White works in the Department of Linguistics and Second Language Teaching at Massey University, New Zealand. She has taught English to adults in Thailand and the People's Republic of China as well as on a voluntary basis as a home tutor in New Zealand.*

*Emmanuel Caussinus at Eurocentres, Alexandria, Virginia USA.*

# Introduction

Case studies can form the bridge between the classroom and the many contexts where students need to use language independently. They give practice in new language and in communication strategies that restore a sense of power when language learners feel that their language is insufficient to make their meaning clear or to be equal partners in a conversation.

# Goal Setting

**Levels**
Intermediate

**Types**
Vocational classes for
ESOL students in a job
training program

**Aims**
Use language patterns to
improve literacy level
and formulate career
plans
Assess literacy level and
foster team building

**Class Time**
45 minutes

**Preparation Time**
30 minutes

**Resources**
Worksheets

In this activity, students read true accounts of a group of students who have completed the course in which the former are now enrolled, find out about these other students, and write about themselves. By reading the supplied text, students think about their own goals and commit these to writing.

## Procedure

1. Begin with a discussion on the meaning of goals, qualities, and attributes and how these affect attitudes to work and the type of work that a student may take up following the course. Elicit examples by writing on board (e.g., for goals, use infinitives). Show that goals, qualities, and attributes must be compatible to be realistic.
2. Show students how to complete the Personal Map Grid (see Appendix A). Elicit examples from volunteers.
3. Have students read the supplied text, complete the Personal Map Grid for themselves, then write about themselves. Give individual assistance as required.
4. Pair off students and have them discuss their writing. Ask for volunteers to discuss the writing of their partners with the class.

## Caveats and Options

1. The supplied text is in the third person. Depending on students' literacy level, assess the need to clarify use of the *-s* ending for present simple third person. Elicit the general rule with examples.
2. More advanced students can write about other class members.

3. As a follow-up activity, you might prepare a handout of student writing from this session. Students could use this as a reading cloze to practice use of the present simple (see Appendix B).

## Appendix A: Personal Map Grid

*Directions:* Read about the students below and then complete the diagram.

1. Luke is from Fiji. He is 28 and married with three children. Luke has done electrical work before. He wants to improve his communication skills and obtain a qualification at Auckland Institute of Technology. When he finishes his course, he wants to study for his Trade Certificate. Luke is a very keen worker.

2. Leti is from Samoa. She is in her forties and has two grown up children. She came to New Zealand in the 1970s. She has worked as a machine operator and as a clothing cutter. She wants to feel more confident in speaking to people in English and to keep up to date with her employment skills. When she finishes her course, she wants to do more skills training at this Institute. Leti likes working with people.

| Name | Place of Birth | Age | Goals for the course | Goals after the course | Qualities/ Attributes |
|------|----------------|-----|----------------------|------------------------|------------------------|
| 1. Luke | | | | | |
| 2. Leti | | | | | |
| 3. You | | | | | |

Write a little about yourself from the diagram.

## Appendix B: Cloze Exercises Prepared From Student Writing

*Directions:* Read about your classmates below. Complete the gaps with the right word.

1. Tony:

   Tony ___ (be) from Yugoslavia. He ___ (be) thirty nine years old. He ___ (be) an aircraft engineer. On the course he _____ (want) to improve his communication skills and after the course he wants to visit employers to find a job. Tony ____ (like) to do a job well . . . .

## Contributor

*Chris J. Clark is an employment skills ESOL tutor at the School of Languages, Auckland Institute of Technology, in New Zealand.*

# Bringing Vocabulary to Life

**Levels**
Intermediate +

**Types**
General and special
purpose English

**Aims**
Understand and use
specific vocabulary

**Class Time**
20–30 minutes

**Preparation Time**
Minimal

**Resources**
Blank cards or slips of
paper for role-play
profiles
Overhead projector
(OHP) and
transparencies

Even when new vocabulary is taught in context, it is more likely to be remembered if the student completes a task using it meaningfully. In addition, students should feel a further responsibility to get it right when they know that their work will become the role-play cards for fellow students. The example used here gives the names for different steps in a process (e.g., buying a house).

## Procedure

1. Elicit the names for the different people you consult when you are buying a house (e.g., real estate agent, vendor, bank manager, government valuer, insurance agent).
2. Explain the work that each person does.
3. Have students tell one another their experience working with any one of these people.
4. Explain that they are going to choose one job and write a role-play card for it. Show a sample role-play card on an overhead transparency.

   | Name: | Fred Quicksel |
   |---|---|
   | Age: | 45 years |
   | Occupation: | Real estate agent |
   | Interests: | Driving sports cars, holidaying with Club Med, collecting prize-winning wines. |

   Reasons for choosing this job:
   > good money, likes contact with people, able to use sports car for work purposes, interest in property investments, wants to become a millionaire by the time he's 50

5. Tell students to select one job and write role-play card according to the headings listed above.

6. Collect the cards and sort them, so that each role is represented in each group.
7. Give the students a particular context for the role play, for example:
   - buyer agrees to buy 14th house real estate agent shows him or her
   - buyer meets vendor
   - bank manager agrees to loan
   - lawyer draws up contract
   - valuer checks property
   - insurance agent agrees to insure property.
8. Have students act out events in a role play using the role-play cards they have received.

## Caveats and Options

1. Students may agree on their own categories for the role-play cards.
2. Students can also write role-play cards to help expand their vocabulary of a particular word form (e.g., adverbs: *cautiously, erratically, skillfully, dangerously*) to describe different drivers.
3. This technique has also been used in teacher education where students write role-play cards to demonstrate their understanding of different teaching methods (e.g., grammar translation, audiolingual, suggestopaedia, total physical response).

## Contributor

*Alison Kirkness is a teacher of ESOL and a teacher educator. She works at the Auckland Institute of Technology, in New Zealand. She has also taught EFL in Germany.*

# A Big Decision

**Levels**
Advanced

**Types**
University

**Aims**
Increase oral fluency in
English through
meaningful role play

**Class Time**
2 hours

**Preparation Time**
1½ hours

**Resources**
Information pamphlets
from an established
AIDS/HIV information
center

Although students may be aware of safe sex practices, they may not have confronted the issue of whether to go for an HIV test or not. For many people this is a difficult decision to make. Playing out the role of deciding whether or not to go for an HIV test enables the students to rehearse complex feelings and attitudes about taking the test. The pros and cons of having an HIV test will provide the dynamic for lively discussion and facilitate meaningful oral fluency practice.

## Procedure

1. Distribute pamphlets that provide background information on taking an HIV test (e.g., *Should I do something about an HIV test?* AIDS Counseling & Education Service, Hong Kong). One pamphlet should be given to each student.
2. Have the students read the pamphlet at home in preparation for the next class. Tell students to consider the pros and cons of taking the test and to reflect on whether they would themselves take the test.
3. In the following class, ask students to sit in groups of three. Distribute role cards, one to the decision maker, and one each to the two decision facilitators (see Appendix).
4. Ask students to role-play an informal discussion in which the student with the decision maker role card tries to reach a conclusion about whether or not to go for an HIV test. The two other students, the decision facilitators, help the decision maker reach a decision.
5. Have groups report back on whether the main character decided to go for a test, briefly summarizing reasons.

## Caveats and Options

1. The role play may be proceeded by a short, brainstorm session in small groups on what constitutes safe sex.
2. The role plays may be followed by an open discussion in which students are free to express their own opinions on taking the HIV test.
3. Role plays may be conducted in pairs.
4. The whole class may do the same role play, or each group or pair may do different role plays.
5. A group or pair could act out their role play for the class.
6. Describe your own experience of taking the test.
7. Be sensitive to which groups of students you initiate this role play with. Students from certain cultural backgrounds may find this role play too frank on sexual matters.

## Appendix: Sample Role-Play Cards

A. Decision Maker

You are a 19-year-old university student.
You come from a large family.
You were educated in a Catholic school.
Your father has a manual job in a large textile factory.
Your mother takes care of your younger brothers and sisters.
Both parents are very conservative about discussing sexual matters.
Both parents believe that their children should be virgins when they get married.
You have a steady boy/girlfriend whom you love very much.
You know he/she has had boy/girlfriends before you.
You believe that he/she has had sex with at least one of them.
You started having sex with him/her a month ago.
You have had safer sex but not safe sex with him/her.
You are worried about contracting HIV and you feel you would like to have a test.
You are worried that your boy/girlfriend will be angry with you if you do.
You are worried that your parents will reject you if you are HIV positive.

B. Decision Facilitator 1

You are an old school friend of the main character.
You are sexually active and you have already had the HIV test twice.
You try to persuade your friend to have the test.

C. Decision Facilitator 2

You are another old school friend of the main character.
You are a virgin.
You think that your friend should not have the test.
You also believe that there should only be sex within a wholly monogamous and committed relationship.

**Contributor**

*Dino Mahoney is associate professor in the English Department of the City University of Hong Kong. He has also taught in England, Greece, and the United Arab Emirates.*

# Problem-Solving Skills
# for the Workplace

**Levels**
Advanced

**Types**
Classes for ESOL
learners working as
professionals

**Aims**
Increase awareness of
own culture and host
culture
Gain skills for resolving
conflicts resulting from
linguistic and cultural
differences

**Class Time**
2 hours

**Preparation Time**
30 minutes

**Resources**
Case studies of
workplace problems

S tudents attending evening classes and their employers often attribute the difficulties these workers face on the job to the students' English language ability. This activity helps students understand some of the other factors that often complicate the solving of these problems, such as personality, cultural differences, and attitudes—problems that cannot be solved simply by improving their English.

## Procedure

1. Explain the steps students will take to complete this activity: Students will be given a case study to solve (see Appendix A). Explain the main stages of solving problems (see Appendix B). Tell them that they will be given a framework to guide them through these main stages. They will work on the problem in pairs for 20 minutes and then in groups of four for 15 minutes. After that, each group will report to the whole class the results of their discussion.
2. Have students choose partners.
3. Give out the case study (see Appendix A) and the problem-solving framework (see Appendix C).
4. Circulate to check progress and answer queries.
5. After 20 minutes, have the pairs form groups of four to compare ideas and to discuss further.
6. After 15 minutes, ask each group to report back. Note their ideas on the chalk- or whiteboard. Discuss possible causes and solutions.
7. Role-play the resultant strategies and linguistic utterances needed to solve the problem (e.g., language needed to describe actions, express feelings, request changes, *I* statement for assertiveness skills).

## Caveats and Options

1.  It is important to develop a positive learning climate in which students feel safe to participate in discussion before attempting to introduce this activity. Students must also feel secure in their identities and have respect for all cultures.
2.  If students are willing to talk about the problems they face in their workplace in class, use these as case studies for the obvious reasons that they are real and more immediate to the students.
3.  If a real case study from a student is used, this student can report on the outcomes of his or her action plan to the whole class after it has been implemented. The whole class can then problem solve the resultant difficulties or negative outcomes.
4.  The time allowed for pair and group discussion as stated above should be monitored and lengthened or shortened according to students' abilities and interests.

## References and Further Reading

Auerbach, E., & Wallerstein, N. (1987). *ESL for action: Problem-posing at work*. Reading, MA: Addison-Wesley.

Baynham, M. (1987). *Action and reflection: The Freirean argument in ESL*. Linguistics and Political Conference, University of Lancaster.

Phillips, S. R., & Bergquist, W. H. (1987). *Solutions: A guide to better problem solving*. San Diego, CA: University Associates.

Shor, I., & Freire, P. (1987). *A pedagogy for liberation*. South Hadley, MA: Begin/Garvey Press.

## Appendix A: Sample Case Study

A trainee doctor from Taiwan has been in New Zealand for 6 months. He has found that instead of being a masters degree student, he is increasingly being pushed into becoming a technician as well. He complains,

> I only had one topic for my masters thesis in the beginning. Now the list of topics keeps growing. Everything seems to belong to my thesis. I can put up with it now, but one day when I've had enough, I'll take off home with the data and they will be in trouble. But I don't care.

## Appendix B: Problem-Solving Process

The Main Stages

1. identify the problem
2. find solutions
3. devise an action plan
4. implement the plan
5. evaluate the outcomes

## Appendix C: Sample Problem-Solving Framework

1. Where is the problem taking place?
2. Who is involved?
3. What exactly is happening?
4. What are the different understandings each person might have about the situation? (List these in the space below.)

People involved and their perspectives

People                          Perspectives

5. How different would the situation be if the trainee were in his or her country?
6. What do you think are the problems here?
7. What do you think might be the cause of the problem?
8. What is the main objective for solving this problem?
9. What could the people involved have done?
10. What are the likely effects of the actions identified in Question 9 if they were carried out?
11. Which actions are realistic and achievable?
12. How should these actions be carried out?
13. How can their success be measured?

*(Note: The questions provided here are guides only. They should be modified to suit the students and particular case.)*

## Contributor

*Trinh Thi Sao teaches in the School of Languages at Auckland Institute of Technology, New Zealand. She has taught ESL and Vietnamese.*

# Character, Context, Concern

**Levels**
Intermediate +

**Types**
Students concerned
with productive skills,
who interact well as a
group, and who don't
mind performing in
front of the group

**Aims**
Perform own written
role play
Use the target language
functionally
Attend to sociolinguistic
language considerations

**Class Time**
Several 1-hour class
periods

**Preparation Time**
20–60 minutes

**Resources**
Props as desired by the
characters

Drama can be based around genuine contexts and concerns supplied by the students. Practicing in class gives students confidence to use the language outside.

## Procedure

1. Discuss how language varies depending on characters' attributes (e.g., age, gender, ethnicity, social difference) and the context of the interaction (e.g., home, in an airplane, at a shopping mall).
2. Brainstorm to come up with two characters, a context, and a concern (see samples in the Appendix). These can be very detailed or quite general. Work together as a class to begin construction of a discussion between the two characters. Perform at least one of the discussion scripts/outlines.
3. In pairs have each student draw a character and a concern strip. Next, have each pair draw a context.
4. Have students brainstorm, draft, and write short scripts to fit their characters, contexts, and concerns.
5. Meet with each pair to check content, organization, logic, and language use before revision.
6. After final editing, meet with each pair again and help them practice intonation, difficult pronunciation, and so on.
7. Schedule no more than two performances per day, if possible. You may want to have the audience rate the various performances and invite another class to a performance by the five best, if your class is interested.

## Caveats and Options

1. Consider performances by several classes in a coffeehouse type format. This could become a popular event for the program.
2. Have students help in constructing character, context, and concern strips, drawing upon their own experiences.
3. These roleplays can also be used for discussion of culturally appropriate behaviors in varied contexts. Students are often concerned about social blunders, and this type of role-play activity can open up frank and open discussion of appropriate and inappropriate behaviors.
4. Videotape the roleplays and conference with pairs after their performances. This time could also be used as an opportunity for assessment.

## References and Further Reading

Donahue, M., & Parsons, A. H. (1982). The use of role-play to overcome cultural fatigue. *TESOL Quarterly, 16,* 359–365.

Fried-Booth, D. L. (1986). *Project work.* New York: Oxford University Press.

## Appendix: Character, Context, Concern Strips

Character

| | |
|---|---|
| politician | struggling actor/actress |
| farmer | hotel manager |
| computer programmer | insurance salesman/saleswoman |
| nurse | secretary for a demanding boss |
| taxi driver | kindergarten teacher |
| worker clothing store | radio announcer |
| police officer | waiter/waitress |
| aerobic dance instructor | tour guide |
| swimming pool manager | bank teller |
| bus driver | auto mechanic |
| doctor | dentist |
| lawyer | |

Context

- You bump into your neighbor at the supermarket.
- You chat together as you wait for an airplane flight to be announced.

- You sit down for lunch together in a crowded restaurant because there are no single tables left.
- You are both watching a baseball game in the local park and strike up a conversation.
- You share a taxi on a rainy day.
- You meet at the hospital while visiting friends who are in the same hospital room.
- You always see each other jogging in the morning and finally decide to speak.
- You sit next to each other on a ferry ride.
- You meet as part of the same tour group.
- A new neighbor moves in next door and you go over to introduce yourself.
- You see a new person in church (or mosque, synagogue) and go over to welcome him/her and to chat.
- You chat with a neighbor while sitting in the Laundromat waiting for your clothes to dry.
- You talk together while waiting in the doctor's office.

Concern

- You enjoy water skiing and fishing.
- You have a big dog that goes everywhere with you.
- You love being near your family and doing things for them.
- You live near a lake and go there on picnics with your two kids and spouse on weekends.
- You love to ride bicycles and sometimes go on camping/biking trips with your friends.
- Your favorite thing in life is traveling. You work hard to get enough money to go on long, exotic vacations. You just went to Greece last year and plan to go to Egypt this summer.
- You enjoy playing the guitar and singing folk songs.
- You're a very good cook and enjoy trying new recipes from other countries.
- You are very close to your parents and brothers and sisters. You're excited because your sister is getting married next week.

- You're leaving for Canada next month for a 6-week vacation. You're worried because you still need to find someone to take care of your 12-year-old cat while you're gone.
- You and your spouse are due to have a baby very soon and are busy shopping for baby stuff. You really want to have a girl.
- You're very involved in collecting money for the poor and never miss an opportunity to further this cause.
- You are a school bus driver and are very involved in volunteer work at your community's elementary school.

## Contributor

*Kim Hughes Wilhelm taught ESL in Hong Kong and Malaysia and is currently the intensive English program curriculum coordinator and assistant professor of linguistics at Southern Illinois University, Carbondale, in the United States.*

# Write Me a Telephone Card

**Levels**
Low intermediate-
intermediate

**Types**
University
Junior College and
Language School
settings
ESOL conversation
classes

**Aims**
Use basic informal
telephone
conversational strategies
and elementary letter
writing techniques
during summer
vacations or other
extended breaks

**Class Time**
50 minutes

**Preparation Time**
20 minutes

**Resources**
Handouts

For some students, the summer vacation is a time when their new language skills have a break, too. Keeping in touch through phone calls or postcards is one way of overcoming that problem.

## Procedure

1. Before students are scheduled for a long break from classes, introduce telephone conversation openers and leave-takings (see Appendix A).
2. Pair off students and ask them to sit back-to-back as they act out the phoning activities outlined for each of them (see Appendix B). Insist that they not look at their partners' handouts.
3. Give examples of how to address a handwritten postcard.
4. Go through summer phoning and writing activity instructions based on those in Appendix C.

## Caveats and Options

1. The success of the writing activity depends on a clear explanation of the procedure; to avoid confusion, the names of imaginary partners are provided in the instructions for this activity.
2. While the emphasis is on informal and rather elementary structures, this activity can serve as an introduction to more complex telephone and writing tasks.
3. Learners may be asked to send the instructor a correctly addressed postcard outlining their plans for the coming summer (or other extended break) before the final class so that address writing procedures can be checked.

4. Some learners may be asked to choose a partner that they don't know too well, and thus feel obliged to do the work.

5. A questionnaire on the back of the handout referring to the vacation can provide an introductory activity for the first language lesson after the break.

6. By mixing partners on the first day of class, reported speech practice can take place as partners summarize their summer conversations to each other.

7. See References and Further Reading for additional dramatized telephone conversations.

## References and Further Reading

Using the Telephone

Griffee, D. L. (1992). *More hearsay.* Tokyo: Addison-Wesley. (American English, see Unit 1)

Jones, L. (1987). *Ideas.* Cambridge: Cambridge University Press. (British English, see Unit 4)

Jones, L., & Kimbrough, V. (1990). *Great ideas.* Cambridge: Cambridge University Press. (American English, Unit 5)

Keeler, S. (1991). *Listening in action.* Harlow: Longman. (British English, Unit 1)

Writing

Swan, M. (1995). *Practical English usage.* (2nd ed.). Oxford: Oxford University Press. (British English, Section 317)

## Appendix A: Useful Phrases for Telephone Calls

# Appendix B: Sample Situations for Pair Conversations

Partner A: Do not show this paper to your partner.

Situation 1: You make a phone call to your wife:

You have a lot of work to do and are going to be late home from the office again. You have to phone and tell your wife why. She is going to be angry, and your excuse must be good. Be imaginative. You must persuade her to finish the conversation with her saying "I love you."

Situation 2: You receive a phone call:

You were waiting for your girlfriend from 6:30 to 8:30 outside the Plaza Cinema so that you could take her to see the hit film *Fat Ballet Dancers* starring Sylvester Stallone and Madonna. It is now 11:00 p.m. the same night and she is phoning to explain why she did not come to meet you.

1. You saw her as you were going home sitting in Pizza Hut talking to a man you don't know.
2. She lives alone, and you can hear a man laughing in the background.
3. You are getting bored with her and thinking of stopping your relationship with her.

Partner B: Do not show this paper to your partner.

Situation 1: You receive a phone call:

The phone rings. It is your husband. He is phoning to say that he is going to arrive home late, again, from the office (the third time in a fortnight). You are a little annoyed because:

1. You prepared his supper an hour ago.
2. He had lipstick on his shirt collar the last time he was late.
3. He sounds a little drunk.
4. You can hear a lady laughing in the background.

You are going to insist that he comes home straight away.

Situation 2: You make a phone call to your boyfriend:

Your boyfriend was waiting for you from 6:30 to 8:30 outside the Plaza Cinema so that he could take you to see the hit film *Fat Ballet Dancers* starring Sylvester Stallone and Madonna. It is now 11:00 p.m. the same night and you are phoning him from your apartment to explain why you did not meet him. You must give him a good excuse and finish the conversation by getting him to promise to take you to Disneyland.

# Appendix C: Holiday Assignment

DURING THIS HOLIDAY PERIOD YOU HAVE TO WRITE FOUR POST-CARDS TO YOUR PARTNER AND PHONE YOUR PARTNER TWICE!

Sample postcard topics and dates for a summer break:
Postcard 1 (July)—Enjoying myself
Postcard 2 (August)—A good trip
Postcard 3 (August)—Summer is a pain
Postcard 4 (September)—FREE TOPIC

1. Each postcard should be at least 70 words long and refer to the topic above.
2. At the end of each postcard, write two key content words (underlined) that you would like to comment on with your partner (e.g., *baseball* and *a date* or *cooking* and *cars*.)

So, what do you do?

IN THE FINAL WEEK OF CLASS, AGREE ON A DATE WITH YOUR PARTNER WHEN BOTH OF YOU WILL SEND POST-CARD 1 TO EACHOTHER DURING THE FIRST WEEK OF THE HOLIDAYS (eg. JULY 31ST)

ARRANGE A DATE AND TIME THREE DAYS LATER WHEN YOU WILL PHONE EACHOTHER

Step 1: Phone your partner Andy 3 days later (e.g., August 3) and:

- ask him for more information about what he has written on the card
- ask him about the underlined key content words
- tell him about the underlined key content words in your card
- arrange a date with him when you will both send the next postcard to each other
- arrange a time and date for him to phone you three days after receiving the postcard.

Repeat the steps above after receiving each postcard. When you receive the last postcard, omit the two last steps (i.e., arranging to send the next postcard and arranging to phone after receiving the postcard). Instead, ask your partner how she feels about starting classes again.

If possible, after the third or fourth postcard, get somebody that you live with to answer the phone and to say, "One moment please."

Toward the end of the summer vacation, photocopy all four postcards onto one sheet of paper and send it to your instructor at the school address.

## Contributors

*Gabriel Yardley teaches English at Nanzan University in Nagoya, Japan. Kaori Miura created the illustrations.*

# Index to Activities

A ll items in the book are cross-referenced here in one or sometimes two ways according to the main focus of the activity. The code that follows (1Co or 2Hi) is to the section of the book and the first two letters of the (first) author's name.

| | |
|---|---|
| Questioning | 1Ma, 1Wi, 3Mc |
| Reading | 1Ev, 1Me, 1So, 1Wi, 2Ba, 3Be, 3Co, 3Jo, 3Le, 3Sc |
| Speaking [many of these also involve listening] | 1Co, 3Fi, 3Sa, 6Al, 6Ma, 7Hi, 7Me, 7Ri, 8Si, 9Go, 9Le, 10Wi |
| Telephoning | 4Ki, 10Ya |
| Text analysis | 2Fr, 2Ga, 2Lo |
| Vocabulary development | 3Ga, 4Le, 6Br, 6Di, 6Mi, 7Wine, 7Wint, 9Wh, 10Ki |
| Workplace language | 5Sc, 10Cl, 10Sa |
| Writing | 2Lo, 3Ho, 3Gu, 3Sc, 4Ki, 4Le, 4Wr, 5Sc, 6Ba, 6Ha, 8Nh |